The Mindful Runner

For my wingman
And special thanks to Hermes and Sebastian for their steadfast support and monumentally helpful insights

GARY DUDNEY

The Mindful Runner

FINDING YOUR INNER FOCUS

Meyer & Meyer Sport

British Library Cataloguing in Publication Data
A catalogue record for this book is available from the British Library

The Mindful Runner
Maidenhead: Meyer & Meyer Sport (UK) Ltd., 2018
ISBN: 978-1-78255-153-9

Aachen, Auckland, Beirut, Cairo, Cape Town, Dubai, Hägendorf, Hong Kong, Indianapolis, Manila, New Delhi, Singapore, Sydney, Tehran, Vienna

Member of the World Sports Publishers' Association (WSPA), www.w-s-p-a.org

Printed by CM Books, Ann Arbor, MI, USA
ISBN: 978-1-78255-153-9
Email: info@m-m-sports.com
www.m-m-sports.com

Contents

Prologue

The Warm-Up

Tanzanian marathoner Juma Ikangaa was a top competitor in the 1980s. Slight in stature at 5′3″ and weighing only 117 pounds, he was a lion at heart and a fierce frontrunner. Other runners knew a marathon with Ikangaa was never going to include an easy first-half pace. Ikangaa would charge off the line at what commentators called a suicidal pace and then wait for his chance to surge so long and hard that the race would be over when he was done.

He came to prominence after winning world-class marathons in Melbourne, Tokyo, Fukuoka, and Beijing. He had three consecutive second-place finishes at the Boston Marathon (1988-1990) before winning the New York City Marathon in 1989 against a field that included Olympic champion Gelindo Bordin of Italy, the then world record holder Belayneh Densimo of Ethiopia, and the previous year's NYC Marathon winner Steve Jones of Wales.

The author fully engaging with the mental side of running © *Rob Mann*

It was a crowning victory for the diminutive artillery major from Africa's Great Rift Valley. His time of 2:08:01 was the new course record, putting to bed the controversy over Alberto Salazar's 2:08:13 record, which had been under a cloud since officials determined that the course Salazar ran was 120 yards short of being a full marathon.

The sight of Juma Ikangaa at his best, the small man out in front of his taller competitors leading the most competitive marathons in the world, was incredibly inspiring. But beyond this image, perhaps just as memorable, was something Ikangaa said, "The will to win means nothing without the will to prepare."

This quote captures so much about the mind's role in the act of running. Ikangaa's will to win evokes what runners come to understand the first time they really push the pace or run themselves beyond their comfort zone. Running suddenly becomes a mental exercise, a test of will power, a measure of mental toughness. The real drama when you're running is going on in your head, not in your quads or your calves, as dramatically painful as they may be.

In a similar vein, Steve Prefontaine, the outspoken Oregon miler who was also a notorious take-no-prisoners frontrunner, famously said, "Most people run a race to see who is fastest. I run a race to see who has the most guts." When Prefontaine says *guts*, he is referring to a mental ability, the ability to marshal the courage, determination, will power, acceptance of pain, and extreme toughness of mind that it takes to run at one's ultimate capability.

It is telling that both runners invoke the mind when they comment on finding success as a runner. They do not make reference to miles run per week, interval speed drills, running technique, workout routines, or VO2 max levels. In fact, Ikangaa broadens the notion of the mental side of running being a key to a runner's success by talking about the will to prepare. Again the role of the mind is brought front and center. The preparation to run your best, as physical as it certainly is, is still dependent on the mental dimension. Can you summon the will to get out of bed in the dark for your first run of the day? Can you force yourself to keep running after fatigue sets in? Can you remain patient through long runs? Do you have the determination to hold your pace as the miles pile up and the training hours go by?

It's All Mental, Isn't It?

The old joke is that running is fifty percent physical and ninety percent mental. Runners recognize the truth behind the bad math in this joke; they don't need any convincing. When I tell people about my first book on running, *The Tao of Running: Your Journey to Mindful and Passionate Running*, I usually say something like, "It's about the mental side of running." More often than not, runners hear that and immediately smile with recognition. "It's all mental, isn't it?" they often say.

What they are referring to, I believe, is the unmistakable mental struggle that takes place when the running gets really hard. You are in the final mile of your attempt to set a new 10K personal record. You hit the final hill just hanging on to the pace you need to succeed. You are giving it everything you've got. Every muscle and fiber in your body is signaling you to slow down and stop but you don't. You will yourself to continue. Your mental toughness wins out. You push on, you hold your pace, you even speed up. It's clearly mind over matter.

There will be a lot in this book about that difficult moment of truth and how to cultivate a mindset that will keep you running when the chips are down and when it seems most hopeless. But we are going to explore a much broader notion of how the mind plays into running, starting from the premise that the mental aspect of running is operating all the time when you run. You may not be focused on what is going on in your head when you're just breezing down the sidewalk, but your mental activity or your mindset while you're running is always of interest.

Mindfulness

A point I make at great length in *The Tao of Running* is that running is a natural fit with mindfulness. In fact, I believe many runners fall into a natural state of mindfulness without even realizing it. Mindfulness can be simply defined as a focused attention on the present with acceptance. By focusing exclusively on the activity you are engaged in, you experience all the impressions, sensations, thoughts, and feelings about that activity very directly and without interference from thoughts and worries about some problem you had earlier in the day or some concern about tomorrow. You try and engage just with the present.

The acceptance part of mindfulness involves those thoughts and concerns that occur to you about the past or future while you are attempting to stay focused on the present. You want to acknowledge such thoughts but not become attached to them. Instead of going off on some emotional tangent about the issue you are having with a co-worker, for example, you let that thought recede while focusing back on what you are doing. You accept the thought, but then you move on.

Temporarily freed from worries about the past and future, you get off the emotional rollercoaster of careening from one problem to the next that often characterizes our thinking, and instead, you experience the present moment with an attention and a depth that is quite uncommon. The result is a reduction in stress, a greater appreciation of whatever you happen to be doing, and an increased sense of satisfaction and well-being.

Now apply that whole dynamic to running. Running provides a wonderfully rich supply of sensations and impressions to focus on in the present. You have the whole world around you to see, hear, smell, and feel, and you have all the sensations from your body generated by the act of running. Stray thoughts intruding on your mind concerning a work problem will stick out to you like a sore thumb. You can easily trap that thought and move beyond it.

The more you stay in the present, just absorbing all the wonderful sensations of running, the more your running becomes a break from the rest of your difficult day.

Similarly there is a lot of shared real estate among running, mindfulness, and meditation. They all operate by pulling you away from your day-to-day stresses and having you focus on the here and now in some fashion. A classic meditation technique, for instance, is to focus on your breathing. You can do exactly that when you're running or practicing mindfulness. All three practices result in similar outcomes: less stress, more appreciation for life, and more self-satisfaction and self-esteem.

All that is certainly good in regards to the positive effects of running on your life, but let's cast an even wider net with this discussion of running and the mind. If you're reading this book, chances are you've already discovered that running seems to do a lot more for you than just provide a little exercise. Running provides a framework for the very satisfying act of setting and reaching goals. There is a social dimension to running. People meet and become fast friends through running. Running promotes health. It is practically a fountain of youth for seniors. In many cases, running transforms people's lives, helping them break addictions, overcome depression, or recover from other severe health or emotional problems.

Quality of Life

Let's consider two more quotes here. The first is attributed to Kara Goucher, a two-time Olympian in long-distance events, a silver medalist in the World Championships at 10,000 meters, and a top finisher at the Boston Marathon. She said, "That's the thing about running: your greatest runs are rarely measured by racing success. They are moments in time when running allows you to see how wonderful your life is." Well-known physician and running philosopher, George Sheehan, said, "The obsession with running is really an obsession with the potential for more and more life." In these quotes, our running sages seem to take the benefits of running to a whole new level. They link running with the quality of life itself.

The point is that when running is properly experienced, fully explored, and deeply appreciated, it can lead you to fully embrace your life and live it to its fullest. At least, that's what I think.

The Mindful Runner is intended to suggest a lot of ways for you to think about your running. Ideally you will learn, among other things, how to enjoy running; see the humor in difficult situations; focus on the journey of running and not the end result; deal with the painful aspects of running; get to any finish line anywhere, anytime, no matter how difficult the race; and deal with injuries and setbacks.

This book stands by itself, but if you want an even fuller discussion of the mind and running, you should read my first book on running as well, *The Tao of Running*. Both books rely heavily on stories to illustrate the points I want to make about the mental side of running. I hope the stories are fun to read in and of themselves. As you read about running situations that I describe, think about yourself in similar situations. Think about what would be going through your mind, what attitude you would have, and what mental strategies you would use to cope with a particular situation. Essentially, my stories are jumping off points for your own thinking about running; they're pathways to finding your own inner focus. I want you to become a mindful runner yourself, not just in the sense of practicing mindfulness as you run, but in the sense of being aware of the role that the mind plays whenever you are running.

My first book, *The Tao of Running,* explores a lot of connections between running and different philosophies such as secular Buddhism, existentialism, Taoism, and the like as well as looking at very practical aspects of the mind's role in running, such as, staying positive, setting and achieving goals, staying relaxed, and using mindfulness to deal with pain. Many of the stories in the book come from the world of trail running and ultrarunning.

The Mindful Runner draws more from the world of marathoning, cross-country running, racing shorter distances (such as 5Ks and 10Ks), and running in general. The focus is more on just exactly how the mind works while you are running and what mindsets and mental strategies are going to help you get through a run successfully and get the most out of every run.

So I welcome you to this world of mindful running. Here are a couple of other quotes that I think will apply as you read through this book. One is by Eleanor Roosevelt: "You must do the thing you think you cannot do." Finally a quote from somebody named Unknown, "Any idiot can run, but it takes a special kind of idiot to run a marathon."

Become a mindful runner and be aware of the role the mind plays whenever you run.

Chapter 1

Running Sucks

Really, unless you're a cheetah or a Siberian husky or a gazelle, your first attempts at serious running are probably not going to go well. Running will reward you in the end, but chances are you'll struggle to get there. You will get sore. Pains will pop up out of nowhere. It will feel like you're not making any progress.

Don't be discouraged. A rough start is common. But help is on the way. Let's discuss a simple mental strategy that you can apply to your running anytime and anywhere. You will use it to defend yourself against debilitating negative thinking. It's nothing new. Quite the contrary, it's one of the ancient heavenly virtues, but we are going to repurpose it specifically for running.

It is *patience*.

One definition I found of patience includes this phrase, "… building a sense of peaceful stability and harmony rather than conflict, hostility, and antagonism." There's a running goal if I ever heard one. Who would not want to run with "peaceful stability and harmony" and not feel "conflict, hostility, and antagonism"? I only wish that when I first began running I had experienced even a little peaceful stability and harmony. Instead, my initial foray into serious running was characterized by a singular lack of patience, and as a result, I concluded that running sucks.

Cross-Country Fizzle

My first day attending Southeast High School in Wichita, Kansas, in August of 1967 was crazy scary. It was a huge school, much bigger than any school I had ever been to before. Right off the bat, I couldn't find my first class and ended up in the principal's office waiting for a secretary to help me out. The hallways turned into a riot every time we changed classes. Some of the seniors looked like grown up men and women. They were monsters. I did, however, manage to find a notice about a meeting after school for those interested in the cross-country team.

I knew zip about cross country. I hadn't done any serious running in my life, but I felt like I needed to go out for a sport. There was the matter of earning a letter jacket, which I assumed was necessary in order to be cool and popular. Only two sports were available in the fall, cross country and football. I briefly contemplated football. I was pretty fast and sure handed. I thought I might make a good receiver, but I was not big. Then I imagined somebody who was big flattening me and that effectively put me off the football idea.

Running, on the other hand, didn't seem like such a big stretch. Who couldn't run? How hard could it be? Plus I felt like I was an

In search of peaceful stability and harmony

okay athlete. I'd played some Little League baseball and had done pretty well. And recently in my last year of junior high school, the school had held an intramural competition in several minor sports. Badminton was one of them, which I'd played a lot as a kid. I signed up and marched through the brackets like I was mowing down wheat. A star basketball player faced me in the finals. He was a big target so my strategy was to whack the shuttlecock into his chest over and over. The basketball coach was laughing, watching me, a little guy, thoroughly confound his best player. I figured I could expect the same kind of success at cross country.

There were about ten or fifteen of us at the meeting after school eyeing each other nervously. We waited for a while. The door opened and in walked Charlton Heston. Okay, it wasn't Charlton Heston. It was Charles "Chuck" Hatter, but he was a dead ringer for the actor. Coach Hatter was tall and had the same sandy hair, prominent forehead, strong jaw, nose and eyes as Charlton Heston. The resemblance was really uncanny. I checked my memory on this by pulling up some photos of Charlton Heston online. Sure enough, one of them was a perfect match with a picture of Coach Hatter in my Southeast High yearbook.

Coach Hatter also had the same commanding presence as Heston, which he used to good effect as both a coach (cross country and swimming/diving) and as a chemistry teacher. When Ben Hur told you to swim extra laps, you swam them. When Ben Hur told you to balance a chemical equation, you balanced it…no ifs, ands, or buts.

For someone recruiting new members to his cross-country team, Coach Hatter had an odd approach. “Cross country is not a fun sport” was the first thing he said. “Unless,” he went on, “you think it’s fun to run up and down hills on a golf course.” That was practically the whole message. It was going to be tough and you weren’t going to like it. He was discouraging us from going out for the team.

Undeterred, I showed up the next day after school for the first practice. We put on our regular gym clothes and got our first look at the juniors and seniors who were on the team. They were dressed in sweatsuits with school logos. They were subdued, quiet, and unsmiling. No one was snapping towels and horsing around. It was not a big party.

Coach Hatter arrived with a clipboard and recorded everyone’s name. Then he told us to follow the juniors and seniors. We would be running over to College Hill Park. I started at this news. College Hill Park was a long way off. It was something like two miles away!

We left at an easy jog and followed an ingenious route through the back streets of Wichita that crossed as few major roads as possible and kept grass under our feet most of the way. The team veterans stuck to a reasonable pace so I managed to keep up with the knot of sophomores running at the back. By the time we reached College Hill, it was the longest continuous stretch of running I had ever done in my life. I congratulated myself that I had made it through my first cross-country workout.

Coach Hatter climbed out of his car as we arrived. I was expecting some kind of acknowledgement of our achievement and then maybe instructions to walk back to the school or board a waiting bus that would take us back. Instead, he pointed to a path that followed the edge of the park, pulled out a stopwatch, and told us to stay on the path "all the way around."

"Ready?" he said. "Go!" This time the team vets shot off the mark and were gone in an instant. It was clear we were supposed to run the mile loop around the park hard. I wasn't halfway around before the fun meter on this running thing had pegged out completely. I entered a state of agony. My legs were like cement. I had a side stitch that seemed to be splitting me in half. My lungs ached and oxygen seemed nowhere to be found. My head was bent sideways from the strain. When we finished the loop, I collapsed on the grass with most of the rest of the sophomores.

"Next loop in two minutes," Hatter said, looking at the stop watch, his calm manner contrasting sharply with the panicked uproar coursing through my head. "Go!" he said.

We went around three more times with only short rests between each loop. I made it, but the last lap was hardly more than a trudge. The workout ended with a two mile "cool-down" run back to the school.

When I got home, I collapsed immediately on the couch. "What's wrong?" my mother asked.

"Cross country," I said.

"Dinner is almost ready."

"I'm going to bed."

The next morning I woke up and experienced something akin to what Gregor Samsa must have felt in Kafka's *The Metamorphosis* when he woke up and found he had been turned into a giant cockroach. My compliant, responsive, comfortable body had become an alien thing. I could barely sit up. My legs were stiff as boards. They were sore to the touch. The slightest movement caused intense, burning pain. I clanked toward the bathroom in a sort of Frankenstein parody. Later, I was stopped cold at the top of the steps when I realized I needed a strategy for getting downstairs.

As I ate breakfast and contemplated day two at my new school, I was sure that I was through with cross country. Of course, as the day went on, and moving around had the effect of restoring me back to something resembling a functioning human, I had second thoughts. There was nothing good about running that was compelling me to rethink my decision, but there was something very bad about having to face up to Charlton Hesston and tell him I was quitting. Plus there were the other runners. I didn't want to look like a wuss.

The wuss argument had won out by the end of the day and I returned myself into Coach Hatter's hands for a second practice. He responded by introducing us to something I had never heard of before: interval training. At first I was delighted to learn we weren't running all the way back to the park but would instead be working out on the track right at the school. No long runs to and from the park, no mile loops around the park. How hard could this be?

We did quarter mile repeats—that is, one lap of the track run at race pace followed by a half lap rest/walk—followed immediately by another lap at race pace, and then the rest/walk again. We did eight cycles of the quarter mile repeats. Then we graduated to half mile repeats.

Returning to the starting point of each repeat after the rest/walk was mind-blowing. I was sure I was finished, couldn't run another step, yet I'd launch myself into the next interval, come back up to speed, and then inhabit that horrible space that was me while I clung to my pace and watched the track slowly turn from curve to straightaway and back to curve. The last couple of repeats at each distance were pure torture. Total mileage for that second day of practice turned out to be just as much as the day before, only it was run at a much higher average pace. I trudged home late that afternoon feeling as awful as I could ever remember feeling.

Looking back now on my cross-country experience, I can see that physically it was going to be a hard slog no matter what kind of athletic background I had. You can't just jump into that kind of difficult running program and not struggle at first. But mentally I was not prepared at all. I had zero strategies for keeping negative thinking at bay and knowing how to deal with the discomfort that hard running creates.

Bring Patience to Mind

As I said at the beginning of this chapter, running doesn't feel that great at first and many people quickly become discouraged. Even if in other respects you're in pretty good shape, you start running and it feels like your whole body is in rebellion, like I felt in my first trips around College Hill Park. There is a process that everybody goes through of having your body adjust to the demands of running. This process takes time. You feel the aches and pains and jump to the conclusion that you are not cut out for running, that you have weak knees or ankles. But if you haven't been running regularly for about six to eight weeks, your body hasn't had time to adjust. You really haven't experienced what it is like to run as a more efficient runner.

This is where a mindset characterized by patience comes in.

Patience is required initially to get out the door every day or two for several weeks even though the benefits of running and any signs of progress may be lacking. I went back to running once after a very long break when I was in graduate school at the University of Kansas. It was the dead of winter and the only reasonable place to run was on an indoor track in the campus's enormous fieldhouse.

Every other evening for three weeks I went there and I'd run exactly two miles, which was sixteen laps of the track. At the end of the two miles I would be utterly spent. I couldn't run another step to save my life. I remember sitting with my back propped against the wall after my workout and watching these two old professors circling the track over and over. They had been running when I got there, ran all through my workout, and now were running still as I prepared to leave. What was their secret, I wondered. It felt to me like I would never get past the two-mile mark.

But the very next time I went to run, my first workout of week four, I got to the two-mile mark and much to my surprise, I felt absolutely fine. I kept going and ran another two miles, sixteen more laps, before I finally stopped. I actually could have gone farther. A little patience in sticking with my program had paid off.

Patience is going to apply to many areas of your running. Long runs, for example, require patience. You want to avoid probably the biggest mistake runners make when they strike out on a long trail run, a half-marathon, or a marathon, to name a few examples, which is going out too fast. After training hard for an event, perhaps for months, the last thing you feel like doing is starting out slowly, but keeping to a moderate, sustainable pace at the beginning, even though you may feel like firing off like a bottle rocket, is the right thing to do.

Patience is required later in a run once you've burned through your readily usable stores of energy and start feeling tired, sore, and weak. A typical response is to speed up and "get it over with," but unless you're near the finish, this doesn't work. Relaxing, telling yourself to be patient, and accepting whatever you are feeling as normal and just part of the process of running will better keep you on pace.

It can be a very long way and you can feel very tired. Patience is required.
© Rob Mann

Even in a desperate situation, like when I was in the midst of doing mile-long repeats during cross-country practice, a conscious effort to be patient would have helped. You can't make the pain and strain go away, but you can cope with it better. Focusing on accepting the situation and being patient as you work through it has the effect of replacing the panic, fear, and self-doubt that would otherwise be filling your mind. You drive out the negative thinking with the positive thinking. It gives you some control over your reaction to the stress.

So be aware of the need to stay patient if you are taking up running for the first time or going back to running after a long break. Consciously bring it to mind when you are reluctant to change into your running clothes and get out the door, when you're struggling through a run and don't seem to be making any progress, or when you're working your way through those initial aches and pains. Use it as a mantra to direct your thoughts away from negative things and back to positive ones.

If you're already an experienced runner, pay attention to how much patience, or the lack thereof, plays into every running situation that you encounter. You might be trying to get through the last couple of intervals in a series of repeats or reach the top of a long climb. You might be struggling to maintain your pace at mile 20 in a marathon or keep up your speed through the next to the last mile of a personal record attempt in a 10K. You might be trying to finish a long weekend run. These are all situations where your body will be begging you to back off and slow down. Fill your mind with the need to stay patient, and you will be better able to maintain your effort for as long as it takes to finish your run.

Chapter 2

The Pride of Wichita

In 1964 in the United States, running was not a big thing. The "running boom" wouldn't get touched off until eight years later after American Frank Shorter cruised to victory in the marathon at the 1972 Munich Olympics and sparked tremendous interest in running back in America. Another five years would pass before Jim Fixx would publish his blockbuster bestseller, *The Complete Book of Running*, and essentially validate and democratize the idea of simply going outside and running down the street.

Running was such an alien concept in Fixx's day that the first order of business in his book was to argue the premise that running was in fact good for you and wasn't going to put you in the hospital or kill you. He had to cite data that women in particular could participate as well without ruining their health or their chances at child-bearing. He was sensitive to the fact that a person running outside in shorts and a t-shirt was still something of a rare sight so he suggested that if you were embarrassed being seen out in public, you could always just run in place in your living room.

Of course, by 1964, the Boston Marathon had been around for almost 70 years and was widely known as the world's oldest annual marathon. Still for much of its history, the race was more a local event rather than the worldwide phenomenon that it is today. Admission was free and the winner's prize was a simple wreath woven from olive branches. Corporate sponsors didn't move in until the 1980s. Women weren't officially allowed to enter until 1972. Katherine Switzer had omitted the fact that she was a woman on her race application and finished the race in 1967 with an official number but not without a race official trying to rip the number away from her and take her out of the race.

And forget about trail running back in the sixties. Trails were obviously for hiking, not running. Wouldn't hurrying down a trail defeat the whole purpose of being out there blissfully communing with nature? Even as Fixx proselytized about the benefits of road running, he couldn't imagine extending the practice to trails. He considered trails too risky because of all the rocks and sticks you might trip on. A few oddballs had been running a race on trails in Marin County just north of San Francisco since 1905 called the Dipsea, but that just proved that people in California were off their rockers. Widespread trail running wouldn't take hold until the 1980s.

James Ronald Ryun

No, interest in running in 1964 around the country was virtually nil except for in one relatively small Midwestern city where suddenly people went bat-shit crazy over running. That place was Wichita,

Kansas, where it seemed everybody and their uncle followed running. People had running fever. The reason for all that interest was named James Ronald Ryun, better known as just Jim Ryun.

History has moved on and a lot of running heroes have come and gone over the years, but it is hard to overstate just what a phenomenal runner Jim Ryun was in his day. His breakout performance came on June 5, 1964 when Ryun was still just a junior in high school. Track meet organizers around the country had noticed Ryun's mile times dropping closer and closer to the four-minute mark. The prestigious Compton Invitational Track and Field Meet of Compton College lured Ryun out to southern California and placed him in a field of top college runners and former Olympians, many of whom had run under four minutes for the mile multiple times.

Ryun got off to a fast start, finishing the first lap tied for second, but then he was bumped heading into the next turn and stumbled off the track. He quickly got back into the race, but a top finish was gone. He eventually closed with the other runners and eight of them crossed the finish line bunched up with only 1.6 seconds separating the winner from eighth place. That eighth place finisher was Jim Ryun in a time of 3:59. Eight runners all going under four minutes for the mile in one race was historic, but Ryun had accomplished something even more special. He had become the first high school student ever to break the four-minute mile.

Since that day in Compton, half a century later, only four other high schoolers have joined the club of sub-four-minute milers. Ryun's achievement stands out from the others in that he is the youngest to have done it, the only one to have done so as a junior, and he would repeat the feat five times in his high school career, two more times than anyone else has ever managed.

A trail marker for the famous Dipsea Trail in California

Ryun's name became a household word back in Wichita where I was growing up just four years behind him. Here was one of our own, a lanky, modest kid with a Christian background making his mark on the national stage. It didn't hurt that his premier event happened to be the mile. In 1964, the one-mile run was an iconic distance in track and field. This was long before the push to bring metrics to the U.S. and switch out all the old distances in yards to the meters used in other parts of the world and in the Olympics. Plus Roger Bannister's dramatic quest in the 1950s to break four minutes in the mile was still part of track's zeitgeist, so Ryun's achievements fit right into the storied mythos of the mile run.

Ryun eventually lowered the national high school record for the mile to 3:55 his senior year. That record stood for an astonishing 36 years before finally being eclipsed by Alan Webb in 2001. Imagine if you were a miler on the track team at the high school

Ryun had once attended and you were curious about what it would take to get the school record? You would have been in for some bad news. Ryun qualified for the US Olympic team at age 17 in 1964. As a high school senior, he was ranked the fourth best miler in the world by *Track & Field News*. ESPN.com recently called Jim Ryun "the best high school athlete of all time."

As a collegiate athlete at the University of Kansas, Ryun started taking down world records. At age nineteen, he held the world mark for the mile (3:51.3) and half-mile (1:44.9). Eventually he also held the world record for the indoor half-mile, the indoor mile, and the 1500 meters, and he pushed the world mark for the outdoor mile down to 3:51.1, a record that lasted for 8 years.

Wichita couldn't have been prouder of her native son. Ryun was known for his extraordinary final "kick." One race after another, he seemed to be trailing badly with a lap to go and then he would unleash a drive to the finish that was unbelievable, vanquishing legendary athletes like Peter Snell and Kip Keino and setting new records in the bargain. But one prize slipped through his fingers and I can remember the intense disappointment felt throughout Wichita when it happened.

Quest for Gold

In 1968, the Summer Olympic Games were being held in Mexico City. Ryun was at the height of his career. He was the world record holder in both the mile and the 1500 meters, and it seemed like there wasn't a single resident in Wichita, Kansas, that did not foresee Ryun coming home with Olympic gold. There was a lot of talk about the high altitude in Mexico City and the effect that would have on Ryun, but the story was that he was training at altitude and would be ready. Plus this was Jim Ryun we're talking about. He always came out ahead. He was the world champion. He had gone undefeated in the mile and the 1500 meter for three straight years, including beating the man who would be his principle rival in Mexico City, Kenya's Kip Keino.

In the 1500-meter finals, Jim Ryun, wearing distinctive number 300, lined up in his usual sweet spot, halfway between the inside and outside of the track. The gun went off and Kip Keino's Kenyan teammate shot out ahead and acted as the rabbit through a blazing first lap of 55 seconds. Near the end of the first lap, Keino moved up to third place. Ryun stuck to his usual strategy of tucking in near the back of the field, biding his time through the first couple of laps and relying on his famous kick to close the gap in the final lap. With about two laps to go, Keino surged out in front. Ryun finally began making his move, but as the bell lap began, Keino's lead over Ryun was considerable. Around the next-to-last curve and down the back stretch, Ryun accelerated and for a short while he seemed to be closing the gap on Keino rapidly.

As Ryun finally began to move up to catch the two West Germans who were in second and third places, I saw in my mind's eye exactly what would unfold. Ryun would burst by the two Germans as he entered the final turn. All through the turn he would be closing the gap on Keino. With just the straightaway to the finish to go, Ryun would pick up more speed. Keino would begin to fade and just like I had witnessed over and over again, the mighty Ryun riding that famous final charge his head wobbling slightly at the top of his tall frame would stream by the fading Kenyan with ten meters to go and win the gold medal for himself and Wichita and posterity.

Except, that is not what happened. Ryun did go by the Germans just as he reached the final curve, but as he entered the curve you could almost see it happen, a chink in Ryun's stride, a faltering. One of the Germans even seemed to pull back up on Ryun's shoulder and Ryun had to redouble his effort to keep him at bay. Meanwhile, Keino had been running strong with long confident strides at world-record pace ever since taking the lead, the formidable altitude be damned.

Instead of fading on the final curve, he maintained exactly the same driving, relentless pace. He carried that speed into the final straight-away and by the time Ryun finished running the curve, there was absolutely no mistaking that the race for the gold medal was over. The gap between the two men was enormous and Keino was driving hard and joyfully toward the finish line. Ryun would win the silver medal finishing three seconds behind Keino. I couldn't believe what I had just witnessed. I felt a sensation in the pit of my stomach as if a large stone had just lodged there. The whole city was going to feel let down, and in fact, Ryun came in for quite a lot of second guessing among sports journalists and just people in general who thought he might have failed in the race tactically, allowing Keino to get too far ahead.

Ryun would later explain that his target for the race was 3:39, a time that he felt would be good enough to win the race. He actually over-performed on race day, besting his target time by over a second and running what he considered the best race he had in him. What he had had no control over was that Kipchoge Hezekiah Keino on that day had simply run a phenomenal race, a transcendent race. Keino's Olympic 1500-meter record set in the punishing altitude of Mexico City would stand up for the next sixteen years. It had been a brilliant performance and not one that Ryun could have easily matched even on one of his best days.

Still, Ryun was young and he would have another chance at Olympic gold. Leading up to the Games in Munich, West Germany, Ryun put in some of the hardest training weeks in his life. He had just run the third fastest mile of all time and was once again favored to win the 1500 meters. But in his opening qualifying round, lightning struck.

Ryun was somewhat boxed in as the final lap approached. As he made a move to the outside to get into position for the final lap sprint, he tangled with another runner. He tripped and fell, his head banging on the curb of the track as he went down. He lay there for several seconds in a daze flat on his back before he was able to get back up and finish the race far out of contention. The crowd cheered him on but his quest for the gold had all ended in that instant when he fell. The International Olympic Committee acknowledged that Ryun had been fouled, but the rules at the time did not allow for him to be reinstated in the competition. Ironically, four years later, the rules had been changed and a successful appeal at those Games would have given Ryun another chance.

Munich was it for Ryun and the Olympics. By then he was 25 years old, married, a father, and unable to continue dealing with his amateur status in the sport. So it was a coincidence that the very year Ryun gave up his amateur athletics career in 1972, Frank Shorter won the marathon in Munich and touched off the running boom back home. Ryun exited the stage just as the stage was being moved to an outdoor theater and enlarged to include the entire country.

How did things start out for Jim Ryun in running? Was he recognized as a running prodigy early on racing around in his crib? Did he amaze the phys ed coach in junior high when the gym class did a lap around the playing field? Curious about Ryun's early running experiences, I discovered a talk he gave on January 26, 2013 at the LA84 Foundation Advanced Track & Field Clinic at Mt. San Antonio College in southern California in which he describes his first encounter with running.

Does any of this sound familiar? He started his sophomore year of high school in a huge new school without any background in organized running. He was shopping around for a sport with the hopes of perhaps earning a letter jacket. In the fall, only football and cross country were offered so after contemplating football, he decided to try out for cross country about which he knew "zilch." During his first workout, he was shocked to find the first task was to run all the way to College Hill Park, which was over a mile away. He had never run more than a quarter mile in his life. The first day of cross country was devastating, and when he went home, he went straight to bed and woke up the next day stiff as a board. He had trouble negotiating stairs to get to breakfast. He told his mother he was through with cross country but changed his mind as the day went on. In the end, he returned for day two and continued on with the team eventually to become one of the greatest runners of all times.

So, yes, except for that very last part, Ryun and I had remarkably similar experiences in our first encounters with running. Our schools even used the same city park as their venue for cross country practice. I went to Southeast but I had actually grown up in the Wichita East High School district where Ryun went to school.

Determination

Our respective starts in cross country were amazingly similar but the outcomes were wildly different. At the same time, I think a common lesson can be drawn from our two experiences having to do with the role of *determination* in running. Jim Ryun had it. I didn't. Ryun eventually showed what determination can do for a runner. I would go on to demonstrate how things worked out if you lacked it.

From that first discouraging cross-country practice at East High to Ryun breaking the four-minute mile and making the US Olympic team, less than two years passed. Imagine the determination and drive Ryun must have shown to make that happen. He had a passion for hard work from the very start and the ability to tolerate the most punishing workout routines. Starting in high school and continuing on through his college years, he was known for the intensity and volume of his interval workouts and for his two-a-day workout schedule. A Jim Ryun interval set, for example, might include 40 reps of a quarter mile. A 90-mile week for him might include 70 miles of interval training all done at a fast pace. His longer runs were almost exclusively what they called "cruise" runs back then, which today we call tempo runs, that is, longer runs done consistently at near race pace.

We've all experienced the situation where it's time for a run but we are just reluctant to get dressed and get started. There is an inertia that holds us back, especially if the plan is to do a hard workout. Couldn't we just skip this one and get the running done tomorrow? Imagine when Ryun got out of bed and was facing two hard workouts almost every day. He would have needed determination just like we do to take those first steps.

Ryun would have also faced pushing himself harder and harder, well after he left his comfort zone during a workout or in a race. In fact, he said the thinking among his teammates was that the workout didn't really start until you got tired. So over and over again in the agony of those late intervals, well into a tempo run, or in competition, Ryun would have had to shut off all the signals coming from his body telling him he was at his limit and push past that and run harder. This was determination writ large.

Consciously bringing determination to your mind as you face difficult situations during a run can help you sustain a hard effort and get through it to the end. A lot of self-talk goes on in your mind as you run, especially when you start feeling fatigued, sore, and stressed. The self-talk can turn negative easily and you can start convincing yourself that you are at your limit and that you need to slow down or quit. In the last chapter, we talked about the importance of maintaining patience and actively using the thought of patience to keep negative thinking at bay.

Telling yourself to stay patient is like a negotiation. It feels bad, but I have to be patient. I will endure this bad feeling for now and see what happens. I will not make any decisions yet. That is patience. Bringing determination to mind is a different animal. It is not a logical argument to give yourself more time and then reevaluate down the road. It is a leap beyond logic.

Determination makes it possible to overcome any obstacle, climb any mountain.

Determination ignores logic. It steamrolls over logic. Determination doesn't care if you think your legs are falling off or you think you've descended into the seventh circle of hell. Determination tells you to keep going no matter what the circumstances and no matter how hopeless things appear. I think it is a defining quality in running because, like it or not, running becomes painful and hard to sustain whenever you push yourself beyond your comfort zone. So every time you run hard, you feel like backing off and there is a need for determination to come into play.

By the way, it's worth remembering that it is natural and normal to feel terrible when you push hard. Everybody feels that way to some extent. It does not signal, though, that something is wrong. On the contrary, it is a sign that you are indeed doing your best and giving your best performance.

Now of course determination has its limits. You may be *determined* to break Jim Ryun's time for the mile or *determined* to run eight quarter-mile repeats in under 60 seconds per quarter mile. Those things probably won't happen. The level of your training is going to dictate just how far and fast you can run. But determination will get you closer to your ultimate potential than caving into the negative voices in your head every time you push yourself. We can all do more than we think we can. But to get to that "more," you have to get past the self-doubt and fear that arise when you think you are at your limit. That is what focusing on determination can help you do.

I mentioned Eleanor Roosevelt's quote in the prologue: "You must do the thing you think you cannot do." Running gives you an opportunity to "do the thing you think you cannot do" over and over again, every time you think you are at your limit but manage to push on anyway.

Actively using your mind to affect your running performance by summoning determination will take practice. The more you work with the technique, the better you will get at it. And be aware of the fact that determination is a mental quality that you are bringing to the service of your running that stems more from the illogical, emotional, subjective, spiritual side of your mind rather than from the analytical and logical side. It's a part of your mind that you want to be able to tap into when the chips are down. It is both unreasoning and powerful.

Chapter 3

To Have and Have Not

It was the middle of the night. Mud-caked shoes, soaked to the bone, shivering, I stood looking at the open door of the enormous white pick-up and asked, "Do you have a towel or a blanket we could throw over the seat?"

"Naw," the stranger said, "just jump in."

A dozen lights glowed from a ridiculously complicated dashboard. The engine throbbed powerfully somewhere underfoot. A blower labored deep in the truck's throat. I fiddled with a couple of dials. Suddenly a flood of warm air that had been trapped behind a closed vent washed over me. It was pitch dark outside except for some jagged slashes of light riding the rain cascading down the windshield. Rain drummed on the ceiling. It felt like I was sitting at the controls of a space capsule, floating above a weird, alien planet.

I was pretty sure I was done. The Cruel Jewel 100-Mile Endurance Run and the rugged terrain of the Chattahoochee

National Forest in the North Georgia Mountains had just been too cruel. The race had begun on Friday at noon. It was now Sunday, about three in the morning as I sat in the truck stripped to the waist holding my t-shirt and shell up to the air stream. The heat, humidity, jagged trails, steep climbs and descents (33,000 feet of elevation gain), ridges, rocks, roots, and 36 hours of running so far had been bad enough, but we'd been caught out on the worst part of the course, the Dragon's Spine, in a cold, windy, lightning-punctuated downpour that had made the trail almost impassable.

Slippery mud now covered the steep little climbs and downward slopes of the trail. I had to search out half-buried rocks to find any footing in the mud and hold onto trees to stay upright. Even so I went down several times, once even sliding all the way off the trail down a slope. All the work to keep moving was the only thing keeping me from hypothermia. The cold and rain had come after I'd passed my last drop bag so I'd left my rain gear there. My shell had soaked through in no time when the storm hit, and apparently the rain had washed the skin lubricant off my inner thighs because a fiery, stinging skin rash there was now torturing me.

I went by two runners laboring together to get up and down the muddy slopes. When they talked, it sounded like they were about to burst into tears. I could hear the frustration in their voices of needing desperately to get to the next aid station, but not being able to make any progress along this trail with the ceaseless rain pouring down, feeling trapped in this dark, wet forest. Time had stopped. Was it two miles to go or six, another hour or three hours?

I had begun shivering and could feel my core heat leaking away. Plenty of times in other races, I'd seen runners succumb to the cold. I'd been there myself, when the shivering got uncontrollable and the only option was to drop. By the time I reached the White Oak Stump aid station, I was right there on the edge.

I asked about borrowing dry clothes, but the volunteers at the aid station had already given away everything they had. Big trash bags to make into a poncho? All long gone. "Okay, then, I'm finished," I said, "unless I can sit in somebody's car for a while and warm up." That's when the aid station captain, bless his heart, took me over to his truck.

I don't know how long I was there. I thought if I waited long enough, the rain might stop. At one point the driver's door opened and another runner jumped in next to me. She was wet but had a decent looking rain jacket with her. She stayed for about 15 minutes and left. I finally had my shirt and shell reasonably dry and was trying to figure out what to do. Of course, I was

Runners, who have no idea what they're in for, starting the race at the Cruel Jewel in northern Georgia

miserable and wanted to quit. I longed to just lie back on the seat and go to sleep. It would all be over just like that.

Going back out into the cold rain looked like a dead end. There were only eight more miles left to the finish but that was going to take hours and hours at the rate I was going. If I continued, I'd be soaked again in about five minutes. Out in the woods there would be no warm truck to save me from a dangerous descent into hypothermia. I peeked out the window of the truck. There was nothing but dark, cold, and rain. If I left the truck, my only hope would be to run hard enough so that the exertion would keep me warm. But running hard now seemed impossible. Just moving was triggering all sorts of pain, not least the awful dragging of my wet shorts across the raw nerve endings in my thighs. I was dead tired, hardly able to keep my eyes open. My stomach was too upset to allow me to eat and possibly refuel. And the way out of here, I'd learned, was a mile-long uphill climb.

Physically, it looked hopeless. But I still had resources, mental resources, and that is why I am telling you this story. If I was going to continue, it wasn't going to be because I suddenly felt good. It was going to be because I could enlist enough patience and determination to keep myself going.

Infinite Patience, Steely Determination

I had a mantra that I had been using for years: *Infinite patience, steely determination*. I used to have to repeat that to myself all the time to ward off negative thoughts and remind myself that, in the end, it was your mind that kept you driving toward the finish.

Ironically, I'd gotten out of the habit of actually having to repeat those words. In the course of running so many ultramarathons, I'd been in so many dire spots and still managed to keep going that it was enough to just tell myself, "Okay, things are bad and I feel awful but, hey, I've been in worse situations. I can still make it."

But my situation in the truck was truly rock bottom. I needed to remind myself what it would take. "Infinite patience, steely determination," I said to myself. I needed to ignore how I felt and ignore my trepidation over the cold.

I struggled into my shirt and shell. I strapped on my hydration pack and stepped out of the truck into the rain. I darted over to the canopy where the aid station table was and thanked everyone for the help. "It's a mile up that trail," one guy said pointing into the dark. "Then it's all downhill to the finish." That last part was, of course, a bald-faced lie.

I turned to face the trail and then wavered. The uncertainty of what the cold was going to do to me was hard to overcome. It was sheer determination that got me moving. It made no logical sense to keep going. Maybe it was even dangerous. So I went to the illogical, emotional part of my mind, took a deep breath, and then forced myself to step back into the rain.

Running uphill on the muddy, slippery trail wasn't happening but I could manage a power walk, striding forward and pumping my arms. In no time I felt the cold rain soak through to the bare skin on my shoulders and then all over. I ducked my head and drove forward, concentrating on my ragged deep breathing. I knew I had to find a balance where I was working hard enough to stay warm but not so hard that I burned through the last of my strength. My thoughts veered back and forth between panic and patience.

The hill lasted forever. I couldn't see anything beyond my headlamp beam in the dark so I had no clue how much farther it was to the top. Time ground down and came to a halt again. Finally I crested Coosa Bald and headed down through Calf Stomp Gap and Locust Stake Gap. The trail turned tricky again, lots of bumps and grinds, rocks, mud slippery-slide areas, and sharp turns. It was work to navigate all that so it kept my temperature up. Near the bottom of the descent the trail flattened out a bit and I made some good progress, but then when no flags marking the course appeared for a long time, I decided I'd made a wrong turn and went back up the trail to find where I'd gone wrong. When I finally found the last flag I'd passed, there was no alternate route there, so it had been a false alarm. I glumly turned and retraced my steps back down.

There is nothing like finding words of encouragement posted deep in the Georgia woods.

By the time, I reached the final aid station on the course at Wolf Creek, which was an unmanned station with just water left out in jugs on a table, the light had come up and the rain had just about stopped. The chill in the air wasn't so sharp anymore. I started to entertain the idea that I wasn't going to die imitating an icicle in the Chattahoochee National Forest.

Of course, my "downhill all the way to the finish" friend had overlooked a final 2.5-mile climb that rose steadily over 2800 feet. But I managed that climb and then dropped down to the final stretch of paved road in Vogel State Park that led to the end.

On that road, an amazing thing happened. Of the four or five runners I could see around me, all limping to the finish, I was the only one running. Sure 42 others had finished ahead of me and almost 40 more would finish behind me under the 48-hour race cutoff, but at least for the moment, I was the cock of the walk. I thought about how crushed and hopeless I'd felt back in that truck. I contrasted that with the joy I was experiencing now as I ran on revived legs to the finish. I clutched the ridiculously over-sized belt buckle that the race director handed me when I crossed the finish line and once again felt the truth in the saying, "You can do more than you think you can do."

A hundred-mile trail run, I realize, is a pretty extreme example for analyzing how the mind can work to help you along or stop you when faced with a difficult running situation. Your experiences, especially if you're new to running, are going to be quite different but the principle is the same. Pain, exhaustion, and unexpected problems pop up and quickly derail you. Your mind goes to fear, self-doubt, and panic. The problem is being able to recognize when this is happening and when you need to stop listening to that negative voice in your head, go elsewhere for a different message, and tap into your inner well of determination.

Dead Last

As I look back on my early running experiences in cross country, I see now that I had little understanding of the whole mental dynamic that applies when you're running. When things started to hurt, I would typically shut down to avoid the pain. That there were good and rewarding alternatives were not evident to me.

Back to my experiences in cross country, after a couple of weeks of training, we had our first meet. Each school fielded three teams: class A, the varsity runners who were mostly seniors; class B, the junior varsity who were mostly juniors, and class C, the aspiring sophomore runners. The A division runners all ran in one flight, B in another, and C in a third so everyone was competing against runners of similar abilities. Modern cross-country courses are 5 kilometers long (3.1 miles), but back then the courses were just two miles.

Not long after the gun went off for my class C race, I could see a pattern develop. There were a handful of runners up front strung out single file, running madly, who were vying for a top finishing spot. After them came the pack made up of most of the other runners all bunched up and jostling each other for position but mainly just trying to hang on and last through the race. Behind the pack came a handful of stragglers who were desperately trying to reunite themselves with the pack and avoid the ignominy of finishing in the last few places.

I found I was capable of staying with the pack without having to push myself to the brink. It wasn't easy by any means, but I could last the two miles and most importantly, keep myself out of the ranks of the stragglers. At the end of the race, when we were all packed into the finishing chute, I noticed something strange. All the runners around me were bent over supporting themselves on the back of the next runner up in the chute. They were fighting for breath, barely able to keep on their feet. Some of them even had foam dripping from their mouths. I was the only one standing there basically unfazed by the race.

It wasn't that I was some kind of superior runner. It's just that I hadn't bothered to run that far out of my comfort zone. Almost everybody else had red-lined it the whole way and left nothing out there on the course. They were totally spent. I just couldn't push myself like that.

I was having a similar experience during our practices as well. Generally speaking, when the going got tough, I didn't get going. I slacked off. Actually, among the class C runners, I was pretty fast. I put down some decent times when we were doing intervals. With intervals, there was really no place to hide, and it was almost impossible not to push yourself. But at the park, I would slow down when we were out of sight of Coach Hatter and give myself a break. Once I even walked a section of the loop where we were hidden by some trees. When I finished the loop, Hatter looked at his stopwatch and told me, "Don't walk in the trees."

So maybe I had some promise as a runner, but there was nothing about the process that I enjoyed. Running was hard, uncomfortable work. Coach Hatter had been right when he warned us in the meeting that we weren't going to enjoy it very much.

A couple of meets later, I found myself in my usual place, back about two-thirds of the way in the pack, in my C division race. I didn't feel great but at the same time I could tell that I had quite a bit left as we rounded a curve and hit the last half-mile of the course. Everyone always talked about having a strong "kick" at the end of the race just like Jim Ryun. For some reason I got to thinking about that. Looking back, I realize that it was probably the first time I managed to avoid my usual negative thinking when the running got hard by flooding my mind with a positive thought.

I was totally focused on the idea that I was going to kick it home. I sped up and lo and behold I found I had another gear. I immediately started passing other runners two and three at a time. I moved to the outside where I had more room and just poured it on. I could hear myself desperately sucking in air to fuel my furious dash. It felt like I had transcended my body, like I was now a spectator or just along for the ride. By the time I hit the finishing chute I must have passed about thirty runners and moved up from buried in the pack to being almost at the head of the pack.

For once it was me bent over and fighting for breath at the end. Coach Hatter was there and he came over and put a hand on my back. "Good finish, Dudney," he said. It was the first time he had ever said anything to me at the end of a race.

A week later, Southeast went to one of the biggest cross-country meets of the season. There were schools from all over Kansas, including all the big Wichita high schools and schools from the Kansas City area, the other big population center in Kansas. The warm-up area where all the teams assembled seemed to take up half the golf course where the meet was being held. There was a PA system blaring instructions and announcing race starts.

Runners were prancing around getting loosened up in sweats with the names of schools I had never heard of. On the bus ride to the meet, Hatter had told me that I was going to be running class B this meet. I didn't know what to make of that. Another sophomore had been running in class B all along, but he was much better than I was. He seemed like a born runner. He was tall and rail thin and had a perpetual grimace on his face like he was digging into the hard miles even before he started running.

Not long before the class B races started, there was more news. There were so many runners that class B had to be broken up into flights based on school size. My flight would include only the biggest schools, that is, the big Wichita high schools, the big Kansas City area high schools, and schools from a few other large towns. Big schools generally meant bigger and better cross-country teams. In my flight, class B was going to be almost exclusively seasoned juniors and seniors with just a handful of top sophomore runners.

We took our starting places behind a curving line drawn at the edge of an enormous flat field. Way in the distance there were two cones marking where the course narrowed down and entered some trees. The idea was that no matter where you started from on the curved line, you had the same distance to run to get to the cones.

The gun went off and in no time I could tell I was in big trouble. Everyone had shot off that line at a dead sprint. I was running as fast as I normally would doing a quarter-mile interval on the track, but the entire field of runners were still steadily pulling away from me as we crossed the field. When I finally got to the cones, gasping for air, there was just one other runner next to me.

The other hundred or so runners were disappearing into the woods ahead of us.

I fought desperately to close the distance between me and the back of the pack, but I couldn't do it. From time to time, a runner or two would drift back toward us from the pack and get my hopes up, but then they'd speed back up and leave my buddy and me alone in the rear. Surely, I thought, a couple of runners from the pack would fade at the end but nothing changed. When we came into sight of the flags marking the finishing chute, it was just me and the one other runner in back. The rest of the field was out of reach.

I sprinted for all I was worth for the finish line. The other runner and I were neck and neck, then I was a little ahead, and then he was. He looked as desperate to avoid finishing last as I was. We neared the line and he pulled ahead. I was last. I stood in the chute behind him and peeked around back toward the finish line. I had this last fleeting hope that I had missed somebody falling behind and that that person would come trotting up to keep me from being last. Of course, there was no one there, just empty space behind me.

I hadn't really cared that much about how I did in the meets or even about my finishing times up to that point, but finishing last was just outright crushing for me. It didn't matter that I was running B or that all the smaller schools that would have fielded a lot of runners in B whom I might have beaten weren't in the race. I had come in last place. In this big field of runners, I was the absolute loser. I couldn't face Coach Hatter. None of the other runners on the team said anything to me but I could just imagine what they were all thinking. How do you come in last? How do you not beat anybody?

The bus ride back to the school took forever. I sat alone, head down, overcome with shame. When the bus came to a stop in the Southeast parking lot, Coach Hatter stood up to make an announcement. Starting Monday morning, team practices were going to be on a new schedule. Afternoon practices were as before, but he was adding a morning practice every day that would begin at 6:30 and end at 7:45. You would then have fifteen minutes after practice to get dressed and be ready for your first class at eight sharp.

The timing and substance of this news couldn't have been worse. To begin with, I was not a morning person. I was a night owl. I struggled to get to sleep every night and then struggled to get up the next morning. Secondly, I hated cross-country practice and I wasn't enjoying anything about running in general anyway. As far as earning a letter jacket, I could see that it wasn't going to happen any time soon and probably not until I was a senior. So that was strike three.

I didn't show up for that first early morning practice. Instead, I quit the team. So my first experience with organized running ended without my having developed any affinity for running or having tapped into any of its rewards. Quite the contrary, it left me feeling totally defeated.

The saga of my letter jacket quest, however, had a happy ending. In the winter, I signed up to be a diver on the swimming team. As luck would have it, Hatter was my coach there again. He kept telling us that we had to make our dives straight up and down so that we didn't get too far away from the diving board on the way down. Finally, I asked him if anybody ever actually hit the board.

"Oh, yeah," he said nonchalantly, "eventually everyone hits the board at least once."

That was all I needed to hear. The prospect of hitting that board was too much for me. I abruptly quit yet another team. Hatter must have thought I was the biggest quitter in the world. Of course later he was going to be my chemistry teacher. It put me off of *Ben Hur* for a lifetime and would eventually color my reaction to *The Planet of the Apes*.

The final disposition of my cross-country career

But since my diving career was so short-lived, I still had time to try another winter sport. I settled on gymnastics. It turned out to be the best fit. I took to it like a fish to water. Before long, I had the jacket. I wore it to school expecting some kind of magical transformation in which I would all of a sudden be popular and cool. That didn't happen. In fact, people acted exactly like I was not wearing a letter jacket and had not suddenly become one of the Beatles.

So in high school I bonded with a sport that was really a young person's game. Most people don't grow old practicing gymnastics. Running, which would end up being a lifelong pursuit offering me endless benefits, I considered a dead letter. If you've had a similar setback with running in your past, don't think of it as the final word on the sport. You should give running another try.

I had not, in fact, become one of the Beatles.

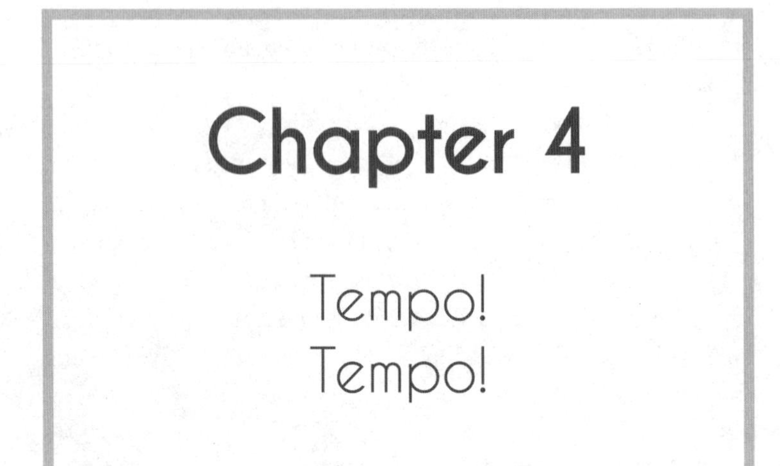

Chapter 4

Tempo! Tempo!

My letter jacket fizzle reminded me of one of my more formative experiences from junior high school. This would have been about 1965 and the number one concern among us teenyboppers back then was being in the "in crowd." We even had an anthem, a song written by Billy Page and performed by "Go Go" (Dobie) Gray that played endlessly on the radio. The catchy refrain, "I'm in with the in crowd/I go where the in crowd goes/I'm in with the in crowd/I know what the in crowd knows" would run through my head all day.

I was, in fact, nowhere near being in the in crowd. Then one day, we were changing classes and I bumped into an old friend of mine from elementary school who was sort of on the fringes of the in crowd. We were talking when a guy who was indisputably, undeniably IN the IN CROWD came up and joined us. He started talking to my friend, but then he actually turned and was talking to me as well. I couldn't believe it. Normally in-crowd people acted like everyone outside their clique was invisible or didn't even exist.

I walked off stunned. What just happened, I wondered. Is it possible that I was in-crowd material? This cool guy had just talked to me like I was not just another underling covered in cooties. My junior high brain went into overdrive. I looked down and watched my feet taking me to my next class. The possibilities whirled through my mind like a tornado in a candy shop.

I got to my next class and took my place in my usual assigned seat. I had my book out and was looking at it but not seeing a thing. The lyrics of the song were going through my mind, "Dressin' fine, makin' time/We breeze up and down the street/We get respect from the people we meet/They make way day or night/They know the in crowd is out of sight." Wow, were people going to make way for me day or night? Was I going to be out of sight?

Then I got a funny feeling. I looked up and the students in the desks all around me were staring at me. I glanced at the teacher at the front of the class and he was staring at me too. In the dead silence, it suddenly came to me that all these people were wrong. These were the wrong students and that was the wrong teacher. I had walked into the wrong classroom and sat down. The girl whose seat I was in was standing there looking at me like I was the biggest jerk in the world…which I clearly was.

Mortified, I jumped up and ran out of there like the room was on fire. When I arrived late at my correct classroom, I had to slink over to my desk with everyone staring at me again. My face must have been ten shades of scarlet. In my own eyes, I'd plunged from hero to zero in the space of about one second. It was a real self-esteem downer.

Self-Esteem Generator

Luckily, I found running, which turns out to be a self-esteem generating internal combustion engine. This is one of the great benefits of running and one worth spending some time exploring and thoroughly understanding. There is no doubt that running boosts one's self-esteem in small ways and in large. You feel the effect after every run: a sense of empowerment and confidence. You feel good about yourself. You feel good about yourself even in the face of a lot of thorny issues that might be weighing you down elsewhere in your life. At least for the time you are running, there is a sort of cessation of worry over problems while you do something for yourself and for your health. A run will even help you gain a new handle on a problem just by creating a little distance between your emotional reaction to a problem and the problem itself. This space increases your ability to keep the problem in perspective and deal with it objectively.

A major aspect of boosting self-esteem is the process of setting and accomplishing goals, which is where running is particularly helpful. When you think about it, setting and accomplishing goals practically defines running. Break down what being a runner entails and all the component pieces involve goal setting and following through.

Your first decision—to make today a running day—sets a goal. Today the goal is to run. Your next goal is to actually get out the door. Oftentimes, this is no easy task. You have to fight off a million conflicting demands on your time, overcome laziness and complacency, squelch that voice in your head that you're already too sore from the day before or that a run today isn't absolutely necessary, and ignore your running partner canceling on you at the last minute. By changing into your running outfit and walking through that door to the outside, you've actually conquered a major goal each and every time you do it.

Then there is your choice of workout and your route. These are goals as well. Is it going to be a hard day or an easy day? Do I go out for a tempo run, a hill run, fartlek, or maybe a trip to the track for some intervals? Maybe my goal is to go long today but throw in some pick-ups along the way. Should I run my usual route or chose something different?

Then we all face the goal of getting through that first mile. Sometimes this can seem like a mountain to climb just by itself. Your muscles are stiff at first. There's no fluidity. The breathing doesn't feel right. Aches and pains pop up and fade away. I make it a rule to not even think about what I'm doing or make any further decisions about the workout until I've gotten past that first mile and all the negative feedback I'm getting from my unwarmed-up body.

Within the workout, there are a whole series of mini-goals. During a tempo run, for example, your goal might be to hold your speed just under race pace tempo up to the halfway point of the run. Then you try to hold it over the back half. In a run with pick-ups, you're constantly picking out a spot to surge to, each one a goal in itself. Another goal might be to get ten pick-ups done during the run, or hold a certain pace between pick-ups. The goals during interval training are obvious. For instance, you set out to do eight half-mile intervals at a pace of under 3:15 per half mile. So there are eight goals to shoot for and a very precise measure as to whether you met each goal.

Every step along the way is another goal set and conquered

And then, of course, your daily workout goals are all part of your broader, more long-range goals like training for your first organized race, breaking your PR in a 5K, running your first half-marathon, going after your first marathon finish, running the Boston Marathon, or crossing the finish line at an ultra event. You might be training to participate in a triathlon or a Spartan event. You might have a goal of running a certain number of miles per week, per month, or per year. You might be maintaining a streak so you have a daily goal of running at least two miles with the long-range goal of keeping your streak going indefinitely.

Running Streak

Streaks, incidentally, can lead to some very odd circumstances. I used to run streaks all the time because it kept me from having to make that decision every day about running or not. I would want to run—I mean, I was really serious about running—but every little excuse would knock me off course and days would go by of me thinking about running but never actually putting my running shoes on and doing it.

My answer was to start a running streak so that every single day I simply had no choice. I had to get it done or I'd mess up my streak. *Don't think about it*, I'd tell myself, *just run*. And that worked for me. Come hell or high water, I would run.

One time I was staying with my sister in her apartment on the edge of a Kansas City suburb out where all the roads were built but all the empty real estate hadn't filled in yet with houses and gas stations and shopping centers. It was Saturday night about 11:00 PM and we'd had a crazy day, so I still needed to run. At midnight, my streak was going to turn into a pumpkin.

I suited up and went out into the cold and dark running around the half-mile square of paved roads where her apartment

The satisfaction of having one more hill climbed, one more goal reached

complex sat all by itself surrounded by empty, weed-choked lots. Pathetic-looking, lonely streetlights were spaced at distant intervals along the road. There was no moon, so between the streetlights the world was dark and flat and foreboding. One of the streetlights was directly above the opening to a sewage drain. As

I approached the drain, I saw that an animal was crouched there next to it. It was a raccoon, still and unmoving, watching me. He let me come right up on him before he ducked back into the drain and was gone.

After making another circuit of the block, I got back to the drain and much to my surprise there was the raccoon again in the same spot and in the same pose watching me. *Didn't he have anything to do?*, I wondered. I took in his black mask, his cute ears, and his sleek fur before I got too close and he disappeared into the drain. The third time I came up on the drain, there he was again. I had a little *Twilight Zone* moment this time when I saw him. It was like he was waiting for me, that I'd entered into some kind of relationship with him. I half expected him to stand up on his hind legs and say something to me. "Excuse me, Old Chap, mind if I bite your leg?"

But then weird got weirder. I looked up and saw a young woman stumbling down the street out of the dark towards me in high heels. She was wearing a little black party dress and had a slim purse slung over one shoulder on a silver colored chain. Where in God's name she'd come from was a total mystery. There was nothing around, no bus stops, cars, people, or anything. It was just me and my raccoon out here.

"Can you take me home?" she said after we'd stopped and she'd sized me up. She seemed a little tipsy and her mascara was running like she'd been crying. I had her wait on the curb while I ran back to my sister's place and got my car. She had me drop her off at another apartment complex a couple of miles away. She didn't say anything on the ride over to her place except to give directions. She thanked me and was gone so I never got the backstory on how she'd come to be out on the streets alone.

I checked my watch. It was fifteen 'til midnight. I drove back to my sister's apartment. I left the car on the street and went sprinting off into the night. I zoomed by the raccoon one more time, telling him as I passed, "No time. Gotta run." I finished the run a couple of minutes shy of midnight, keeping my two-month-old streak intact.

Incidentally, the world's longest recorded running streak belongs to Ron Hill of Great Britain who ran at least a mile every day for over 52 years. In fact, there is an Official USA Active Running Streak List maintained by the United States Running Streak Association, Inc. To get on the list, you have to have a certified streak of at least one year in duration. There are 787 names listed. The first fifteen people on the list all have streaks surpassing 40 years. Talk about having a goal!

Of course, there will be times when you miss a goal. You're ready to go after your 10K record and you have a bad race and fall short. You get halfway through your first marathon and an ankle issue takes you out. This is all part of the process. Falling short of a goal is just evidence that you're putting goals out there that are worthy of your best efforts. Tom Hanks embodied an old notion about goals in the movie *A League of Their Own*, when he explained to his all-women baseball team, "It's supposed to be hard. If it were easy, everyone would do it." Thomas Paine expressed much the same idea when he said, "What we obtain too cheap, we esteem too lightly: it is dearness only that gives every thing its value."

Missing that 10K record on that day might have been the best thing that ever happened to you. It will motivate you to train harder the next time around and come back stronger. It will lead you to rethink and reset your training goals along the way.

You'll feel good about yourself that you were knocked down but that you got back up and are now fighting on to try again. And finally there is nothing like the satisfaction you will feel when you get another chance at that 10K record, pour out your best effort, and succeed where you failed before. It often takes that initial failure to elevate the accomplishment of a difficult goal to a life affirming moment.

Reaching for the Stars Polish-Style

And speaking of life-affirming moments, I am reminded of when I was a Fulbright Exchange Lecturer in Poland teaching English as a Second Language back in the late 1970s. Of course, Poland was a communist country back then. I ran a discussion group with some Polish professors who were working on their English language skills and the topic of conversation was often about how frustrating and unfulfilling Poles' professional work lives were. The communist system made such a mess of things that essentially very few were motivated to work hard and excel at their jobs because those things just weren't well-rewarded. Generally speaking, people just put in their time at work and waited until they could go home. On the face of it, visiting shops or offices, it looked like Poles were listless, surly, indifferent workers.

But Poles had somewhere else to put their time and energy. They organized social clubs that operated somewhat independently of the government. There were sailing clubs, skiing clubs, knitting clubs, language clubs, running clubs, singing clubs, embroidery and sewing clubs, and a club for just about anything you might

Giving up during this race made it possible to return and savor my success even more than if I had finished the first time.

want to do in your spare time. I just assumed that these clubs were sort of relaxed affairs where you could get away from the hassles of everyday, bleak communist existence and enjoy yourself a little.

One day, my wife had the idea that we should join a ballroom dancing club and learn how to jive and foxtrot. It sounded like fun so off we went. What we experienced was basically the ballroom dancing equivalent of Navy Seal training. The instructor and his partner were competing in European-level dance contests. The better club members entered national competitions within Poland. Every practice was long, rigorous, and exacting. From day one, you were striving for absolutely perfect form in every dance. The men were like automatons endlessly repeating perfect steps. The women followed suit, perfect steps and exact gestures down to their fingertips. They looked like they went home and drank blood. For the Viennese waltz, the couples were clamped together at the pelvis with their upper bodies leaning away, heads turned, everything above the waist stiff as boards. Below the waist, their legs frantically plunged and rose, twirling their conjoined bodies in perfect circles, flowing around the room in uncanny unison.

It took no time to understand that the dance club wasn't for fun at all. It was an outlet, a chance for the dancers to realize their potentials, to rise above the frustrations of daily life, to reach for the stars, and infuse their lives with meaning. I went on to discover that this was typical of Polish social clubs. Deprived of putting their energy and their passion into their working lives,

Poles tended to tell it like it is. This sign warns, "Beware of the dog and that's no joke!"

Poles poured themselves into these alternate pursuits where they could express themselves more fully and have the satisfaction of reaching for and attaining lofty goals.

I used to go out for jogs around the city where I lived. I was all alone out there. The running boom hadn't reached Poland at the time so the sight of someone jogging down the street in Wroclaw was quite peculiar. I wasn't training for any races or for anything in particular. I was just out maintaining my fitness so I was never running very hard. As cars passed by, drivers would often roll down their windows and shout at me, "Tempo! Tempo!" They were telling me to speed up.

I believe the reason they did that was because Poles would have been thinking about running in the context of a running club, and I'm sure the running done in a running club followed the same pattern as the dancing in the dance club. In other words, full throttle at all times or else why were you even bothering to run? The sight of someone jogging down the street who wasn't pushing him- or herself to the brink would have been just too hard to pass by and not remark on. The Poles shouting at me weren't putting me down; on the contrary, they were encouraging me to reach for lofty goals and not settle for mediocrity.

Chapter 5

Night on Topatopa Bluff

Never underestimate how far setting a goal can take you and how strange and amazing the adventure can be reaching that goal. A case in point for me and my running buddy Rob Mann was trying to earn a belt buckle for completing a race called the Coyote Two Moon 100 Mile Run in the mountains above Ojai in southern California.

It was a remarkably difficult race which entailed climbing up to the top of a 5000-foot-high ridge and then back down over and over on a system of rocky, technical, and, dare I say, godforsaken trails. We had done the 100-kilometer version of the race twice and vowed to each other several times that we would never, ever enter the 100-mile race. The 100K there was so hard, it took us 19 hours to finish it at a time when we were running other 100Ks in only 13 hours. The 100-mile course looked impossible.

But of course we were stupid and this brings me around to the quote that you may recall from the prologue: "Any idiot can run, but it takes a special kind of idiot to run a marathon." Well, in this case, it took a couple of special kind of idiots to go to Southern California and try to run the 100-mile version of the Coyote Two Moon. Somehow going down there and finishing the 100-mile course had become our *raison d'être*.

Rob couldn't make it the first time we were going to attempt the 100 mile, so I was there alone and endured a full-blown blizzard slamming into the ridge as the race was in progress. Conditions were so bad that the race director had to call off the race and then scramble to get everyone to safety. Runners were scattered all over the ridge, including me. (You get the whole story of this misadventure in *The Tao of Running*, by the way.) No one officially finished the 100-mile race that year. No finishers and thus no buckles.

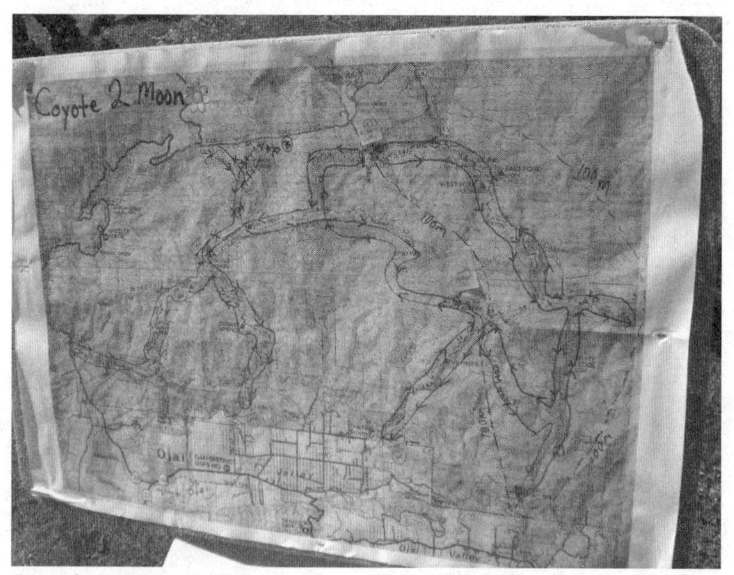

Race director's map of the course at Coyote Two Moon. Each out and back includes miles of steep climb.

Actually, the race was sort of in its death throes by then and that year was supposed to be the last running of the race. But with all those disappointed runners, who, like me, dreamed of getting a buckle there but saw what was going to be their last chance disappear in the snow on the top of the ridge, Chris Scott, the race director, took pity and extended the race for one more year. Rob and I were delighted. We couldn't believe we were getting another chance. By then we'd spent so much time thinking about the race that we'd essentially begun equating finishing the Coyote Two Moon with preserving our manhood. Nothing short of winning the buckle was going to do.

So naturally we arrived at the final running of the race keyed up like a couple of piñatas, ready to burst open and spray treats all over the mountains. Long story short, we then proceeded to blow it. Rob went running down the wrong trail off the ridge and lost so much time that he got discouraged and dropped out. I pulled into an aid station freezing cold in the middle of the night and couldn't for the life of me get warmed back up even under a couple of blankets. My mind was too dull and wiped clean from the struggle to think straight. Jumping into a car to warm up and then trying to get back into the race never even occurred to me. I just wanted to go home, so I quit as well.

We drove home the next day about as miserable as we could possibly be. We'd had our golden opportunity. We were both there, ready to go. We were trained. We were healthy. All we had to do was run a hundred stupid miles, but we failed. And there was never going to be another chance.

Or was there…

The Very Last Chance

Every step promised disaster. I placed a foot in the loose grit on the steep slope in the crook of the next switchback and shifted my weight slowly to see if it would hold or if I would go sliding off Topatopa Bluff taking the loose stones that marked the edge of the trail with me. I looked up. My headlamp flashed over an endless jumble of rock debris that seesawed back and forth up the mountain. The trail was a narrow slippery ribbon threading up through the loose stones, and somewhere beyond where my light failed was Vicki's Memorial, where I would leave the stone I was carrying and then be allowed to return to Earth.

If it had been daylight and I had been feeling human, this trip up Topatopa might have been manageable, but I was slammed. Rob and I had been running since four o'clock Friday afternoon. It was two o'clock Sunday morning, so this was our second night on the trail with no sleep and little rest, except when we occasionally flopped down in the dirt on the trail unable to continue and closed our eyes for a restless moment.

Besides being dead-tired, exhausted, and catatonic, I was parched. My water had given out long ago. Rob and our pacer David Nakashima, who was with us on our final twenty-mile loop, had water, but I figured I would just drain their supplies and still be thirsty, so I was sucking it up. Meanwhile, painful blisters on both heels were exploding with each step, and my stomach had gone south so I was bent over and dry heaving and wishing I could just throw up and be done with it.

Suddenly rocks came tumbling by me dislodged by Rob tripping and sliding down the trail. He had been leading the way up the mountain. "I'm not going up there," he growled.

"Where's your rock?"

"I left it there." He pointed up to a rock formation about twenty feet above us. "It's another mile to the top. I'm not doing that. *He* said we could tell our own story. Well, this is my story. I'm not going up there."

I carefully braced my feet and straightened up so I could look farther up the mountain. I didn't want to tumble over backward. Beyond the rock formation, there were many more switchbacks disappearing over a rim high above. The weight of the ninety miles we'd covered to get here seemed to settle on my shoulders. I shifted beneath the straps of my hydration pack. My head ached. My feet hurt. My stomach was a mess. My legs had been dead for hours.

We were here because it was my sixtieth birthday. I was determined to do something to thumb my nose at this venerable milestone. I needed to prove that I was turning sixty but I wasn't getting old. I had looked at a lot of 100-kilometer races, thinking that a 62-mile run for my sixtieth birthday would be just the thing. But somehow that didn't seem like enough. In the past few years, I had become a dedicated ultrarunner. I reasoned that with ultrarunning, you should go big or you should go home. A hundred-mile race, I decided, was just what I needed to really goose that venerable milestone in the butt.

At the same time, the unrealized goal of finishing the Coyote Two Moon 100 was stuck in my craw. If only we had another chance. Then it struck me like a cicada slamming into my forehead on a warm summer evening. What if we did the race ourselves? Do it right on my birthday! I could kill two birds with one stone, thumb my nose at turning sixty and put the big kibosh on this Coyote Two Moon curse. There was even going to be a full moon, a standard Coyote Two Moon prerequisite, on the weekend of my birthday in October.

We checked in with Chris Scott, the past director of the race, and got his blessing. The course was all public park land so we were free to do whatever nonsense we wanted to there as long as we didn't burn the place down. Scott even offered to send us a couple of leftover Coyote Two Moon finisher's buckles should we succeed so not only would we have the satisfaction of finally conquering the course, we would have the hardware to put in our trophy cases.

We enlisted Robert Josephs and David to help as crew, so we were all set to run the race as a little self-supported unit. Well, we were set after planning the whole thing, making hotel reservations, pulling together all the equipment, buying food, getting everyone down there, and working out how our two-person crew was going to recreate six major aid stations all by themselves working out of the back of a mid-size SUV. It seemed like Napoleon had less to worry about invading Russia.

But eventually at four o'clock Friday afternoon on October 26, Rob and I duly left the Rose Valley Falls Campground and headed up the Rose-Lion Connector Trail on the first leg of our 100-mile solo journey feeling equally exuberant and apprehensive. Right away it was hard to follow the trail. We had a map that gave us the broad outline of our route, but the trail didn't want to cooperate. It wandered around through landscape that didn't look familiar to us at all even though we'd been there before, shot up a slope

Documenting the start of our little adventure, which we called the Coyote Two Moon Redemption Run © *Rob Mann*

when we thought we should be down in a valley, shot down a slope when we thought we should be escaping the valley, split into two directions, and then just seemed to disappear. It was obvious that we had overestimated our familiarity with the trail and underestimated how much the trail markings that were there during the actual race had helped with navigation.

At one point after it got pitch-black dark, we were in the woods and found ourselves clambering over a jumble of rocks following a dried-up stream bed. It didn't seem right so we stopped and pored over our topo map looking for clues. It did look like the trail and the stream converged so we talked about committing to the stream bed. Maybe it turned back into a trail farther down, we surmised. The stream eventually had to connect with the road we wanted. I looked down the long dark tunnel of the streambed falling away through the woods and the jagged boulders we'd have to scramble over.

We'd already backtracked two times looking for where we might have gotten off the trail, but with no luck. We kept ending up at the steam. We decided to try backtracking one last time. This time Rob ducked under some low hanging branches that were on our right. I followed and our lights lit up a solid bank that looked like a dead end, but we could just make out an incline angling up the bank. A few steps up the incline and there was the trail as clear as day. A toppled tree had obscured the correct route and almost cost us the whole venture. The trip down the streambed would have been a disaster. It would have been miles of bushwhacking, and we probably would have triggered our three-hours-late alarm that stipulated that our crew would call for help if we overshot our projected time by that much.

Back on jeep roads and a more familiar part of the course, we sailed down to the bottom of Sisar Canyon where David and Robert had the first aid station set up. We languished in their experienced care and picked over the supplies of sandwiches, soup, chocolate, soft drinks, and water. The whole venture started to seem like a good idea again.

Recharged we loaded up with plenty of food and water and set out to climb back up onto the ridge. From the top of the ridge, we would shoot down Horn Canyon Trail once more to the bottom in Ojai. This was the nature of the beast. Climb up the ridge, follow the road along the top for a while, then drop all the way to the bottom. Then back up, again and again.

After Horn Canyon, we reached the top of Gridley Trail back atop the ridge at three in the morning and were met by ribbons strung across the trail entrance. A notice tacked up there informed us that just six days earlier a bear had attacked a woman who had apparently surprised the bear and its cub lower down on this trail. The trail was closed for two weeks. So we had no choice but to skip it and go on to the next trail to get down off the ridge. We figured we'd make up the distance somehow later. Of course, it was not ideal that a pissed-off mother bear was running around out there. Had she gotten the memo that she was supposed to stay on the closed trail and not wander over to all the other trails where we were? I doubted it.

We reached the bottom of Pratt Trail at a place called Cozy Dell just as Saturday morning broke. Cell phones worked on this side of the ridge so we'd called ahead to David and Robert about the bear-induced change in plans. They were waiting with hot soup, coffee, sleeping bags to throw over us, and camp chairs to settle into. The morning light always gives all-night runners a surprisingly big boost, so after a brief nap, we blasted back up the trail ready to rumble. From there it was a brutal seven-mile climb to get back up on the ridge and then a couple more miles to get to the next trail down, Howard Creek Trail. This one we doubled up, going up and down twice to get back most of the distance we'd lost by skipping Gridley Trail.

We killed the whole day on the Howard Creek Trail loops and then getting back over to the start/finish at the Rose Valley Falls Campground. We were at about eighty miles at this point and faced a big twenty-mile loop back onto the ridge and then around to the trails where we'd started. While we were on the loop, there would be no more aid stations and part of the course was an out and back to the top of the Topatopa Bluff.

Discovery of the sign warning of the bear attack. Gridley Trail is closed. Now what do we do? © *Rob Mann*

Night had fallen once again on our little enterprise, and things had gone a little grim. We had picked up David as our pacer for the final loop but the excitement of having him along didn't last long. There were several false summits on the climb up Rose Valley Road, which kept fooling me, so by the time we got to the actual top, I was feeling discouraged.

Earlier in the run, I would anticipate a landmark and quick as a bunny it would be there. Now the landmarks would not come. My anticipation would turn to despair as nothing appeared, then to hopelessness, then to anger, and it would go on and on, until I got beyond hope or longing or desire and became numb to it, and still it would not come, and I would trudge on and on, and only then finally would it appear. But by then reaching the goal was inadequate. Nothing could fill the void left by the long struggle to get there. That's how the loop was going.

On Topatopa Bluff

Back on Topatopa Bluff, I pushed past Rob and muttered, "I'm going to the top." My one coherent thought was that everyone who had finished this course before had made this climb. As far as I was concerned, no story about finishing Coyote Two Moon was going to be complete without the top of Toptopa being part of it. Rob disappeared behind me. I clawed my way up the endless trail until finally out of the dark it appeared, a big flat stone just in front of a large pile of rocks, Vicki's Memorial. I placed the tiny rock I had brought with me on the flat stone and sat down.

I wasn't there long before Rob appeared. He had changed his mind, but now he was overcome by some kind of monumental hissy fit. He flung his rock down and told me he really ought to be shoving the rock up my ass and that he felt like shoving all the rocks on the whole mountain up my ass. It's possible that he also said that when we got back down he was going to shove David up my ass, too, but happily I wasn't following his logic. I was in such a deep funk stupor from the whole thirty plus hours of running that I was registering almost nothing mentally. First of all, I didn't get why he was mad specifically at me. Secondly, I had other fish to fry.

Ooze Here, Ooze There

By the time we got down off the steep slope and on to the last five miles of single track to the finish, I had stopped functioning independently. I was like a child. I was just dumbly tagging along, going wherever everyone else was going. My thinking was on par with that of an amoeba: ooze here, ooze there. Meanwhile Rob had gotten himself into such a lather back on the mountain that now he seemed to be operating on pure adrenaline. He was flying down the trail, which was suddenly taking an ominous route along the edge of several cliffs. David and I could barely keep up with him.

From time to time, the confusion in my brain would coalesce around a question. I would yell out, "Are you sure this is the trail? Are we going the right direction?" Rob would stop and we'd huddle around the map, which indeed showed that there was only one trail and we had to be on it and going in the right direction. My pea brain would register that, but five minutes later I'd be asking again, "Is this the right way?" Luckily, Rob had become the adult to my child. He kept us moving and on course.

At last we descended to the bottom of Lion Canyon, got beyond the cliffs of death, and came to the last trail junction, which put us unmistakably back on the map and on the right route. We had less than two miles to go. Our new problem was that, down on the valley floor, it felt like we'd stepped into a deep freeze. I struggled into the warmer jacket, hat, and gloves that I'd been carrying all night.

It started to get light but we were back in the area where the trail was hard to follow. The growing light revealed a weird, unfamiliar landscape of scrub and mesquite and sandy ridges and dead trees. The trail disappeared up a naked, rutted ridge of red sandstone that didn't look at all right and we came to a halt, convinced once again that we were lost. Instead of being just a few minutes from finishing, we imagined we had gotten sidetracked into some lost canyon and were probably headed for Nevada rather than the parking lot at Rose Valley Campground. We tried back tracking but the only semblance of a trail was what we were on so we turned around and followed it and hoped for the best.

When we reached some high ground, we could see the Rose Valley Road climbing the ridge in the distance so at least we knew we were going in the right direction. We recommitted to the mystery trail and after what seemed like forever, we saw the trailhead where it had all begun, the finish, though we seemed to be coming at it from the wrong direction. Whether we actually got back to the finish on the right trail is not clear, but our guess is that we ended up getting back the rest of the distance we'd lost when we were forced to skip Gridley Trail.

We stepped out onto the black top and saw our car parked across the road. Robert appeared and took a picture of the strange, furtive gesture we made to mark the end of our journey. It was not a handshake or a high five. It was our fists held downward close to one another. No one knows where that came from or what it meant but it captured the moment.

Strangely, having arrived at the end, I felt no joy. I was so beaten up I wanted to cry. It seemed that I had visited such a deep and dark place out there on the trail that I hadn't come all the way back yet. That was going to take some time. We sat in the warm car with blankets over our laps and got used to the idea that we were done. We had been running for 39 1/2 hours. We'd covered about one hundred miles, maybe more, maybe slightly less. Neither of us doubted, though, that we had put in a complete and

The actual furtive gesture at the end of the run. What could it mean?

© Robert Josephs

honest Coyote Two Moon 100 mile effort and deserved to claim the belt buckles even if we had been forced to follow a modified course.

Why had this particular goal become such an *idée fixe* for us among all the possible running goals we might have imagined? I don't know. It just grew organically out of circumstances. First, we had originally thought of 100 miles at Coyote Two Moon as impossible so that was sort of a thumb in the eye to begin with. Then there was the *in medias res* cancellation, followed by our combined screw up at the last official running of the race.

In many ways, it had become the perfect goal. It was distant and hard and required us to stretch ourselves beyond our own imaginations. Achieving the goal would take growth, stubbornness, will power, and determination. And reaching the goal after repeated failures was going to make it even sweeter, even more satisfying than if we had accomplished it the first or second time around.

Immediately after finishing, it is true, I felt more crushed than triumphant. Both of us had been forced into rocky new psychological territory. Rob had tapped into an anger that had lifted him past all the other physical and mental barriers out there. (It was actually a mechanism that I had discovered and used to good advantage in a different 100-mile race, which is another story you'll find in *The Tao of Running*.) The anger might have been partly directed at me for alternately being so stubborn and then so helpless, but I'm sure it was more anger at the desperate situation we were all in. Whatever the target of the anger, it

And here's the long sought-after buckle to prove it. *© Rob Mann*

brought him out of a low point and transformed him into a super runner when it really counted.

I was amazed to discover in myself a whole new state of mind out there. Let's call it functioning helplessness. It felt like I couldn't do a thing for myself. Alone, I would have just sat there like a rock, but as long as someone was leading the way, I was perfectly capable of following and not quitting. Near the end, when we were lost, I was no help finding our way out, but again, as soon as someone had an idea where we should go, I was up and ready to get there. I had never experienced that state of mind before and haven't experienced it since, but it's like a tool tucked away back in my mental toolbox. I can be broken in about every way, but I can still keep going as long as I get a little guidance.

Looking back on the whole adventure, it's one of the most memorable things I have ever done. And it all happened because we set a goal and we were determined to accomplish it.

Chapter 6

To the Stars Through Difficulty

State mottos would seem like an odd place to look for insights into the mental side of running, but my home state of Kansas actually has a motto that is quite relevant to the discussion. In fact, it could practically serve as a motto for running itself: *Ad astra per aspera* or "To the stars through difficulty."

The motto is aspirational. "To the stars" denotes reaching for an uncommonly high goal. It implies a desire not just to get by in life but to lead a remarkable life. Running can help us do just that. John James Ingalls, who suggested "To the stars through difficulty" as the state motto, believed people living in Kansas in the 1850s were determined to build a notable society. He wrote that "the aspiration of Kansas is to reach the unattainable; its dream is the realization of the impossible."

His use of the words *unattainable* and *impossible* probably stemmed from the dire situation that Kansas was in at the time.

The contrast between the peaceful and productive society that Ingalls saw Kansans aspiring to and the horrifying reality of the conflict over slavery, which had engulfed the state for years even before the Civil War began and earned it the name "Bloody Kansas," must have indeed made a harmonious society seem far out of reach.

Moreover, beyond this raging open war over slavery, just about every other aspect of settling in Kansas exemplified difficulty. Many homesteaders moving west chose Kansas for its rich farmland, but the tallgrass prairie did not yield easily to the plow. The climate was harsh, marked by tornadoes, blizzards, drought, hail, floods, and just general unpredictability, so losing crops was common. Grasshoppers and other pests could destroy crops as well. The farm work was oppressively hard. A single person couldn't manage, so the whole family had to pitch in to cover all the chores.

To add to the settlers' dilemma, Native Americans were being relocated to Kansas from the east. Broken treaties, misunderstandings, and competition for the resources of the land practically guaranteed a constant state of tension between Native Americans and early settlers leading to conflict, recriminations, and bloodshed. When Kansas did finally enter the Union as a free state, a large contingent of her men immediately went off to war. The loss of men from Kansas who were killed or died of other causes during the Civil War turned out to be greater per thousand than from any other state in the conflict.

Thus "to the stars through difficulty" was not a superficial slogan for the state but rather a uniquely accurate characterization of the enormous struggle that people in Kansas were engaged in and a rallying cry for people who were faced with mind-numbing challenges to nevertheless aim for a transcendent future.

It's often noted that running is a very natural activity for human beings; that in fact, we are uniquely evolved for the purpose of running and running efficiently. That makes it sound like running is going to be easy for us, like falling out of bed. We have all heard of the role that endorphins play in running and the pleasant-sounding "runner's high" that endorphins supposedly create. There is also the concept of flow and the notion that running, even at high levels, can seem effortless, that time and distance can flow by unnoticed, that the runner can "float" through a workout.

Okay, well, hold your horses. All that cushy-sounding stuff applies to running to one extent or another but with a lot of complicated caveats. The more basic and applicable fact is that running, generally speaking, is hard, and it gets harder the more you pursue improving at it. That is not to say that it is uniformly unpleasant and that you can't work up gradually and spend a lot of your time running in your comfort zone, but you are not going to avoid experiencing some pain and suffering if you want to go faster, run farther, or reach toward achieving your highest potential as a runner. We've all heard the pithy aphorism that embodies this reality: "No pain, no gain."

Pain and suffering are going to be a part of the picture of your running so it is worth coming to grips with this notion and realizing that it is the overcoming of these difficulties that lead you to the rewards that running offers. The feeling of accomplishment, the boost in self-esteem, the sense of being able to tackle other difficulties in your life are all outcomes of facing

With running, there is going to be pain and suffering.

down the suffering and winning through to your goals. It is the path through difficulty that leads you to the stars.

It's also worth noting that you have a lot of say in just how you react to the pain and suffering that you are going to inflict upon yourself as you train. As the anonymous saying goes, "Pain is inevitable, but suffering is optional." I don't really buy that suffering is optional in the sense that you can escape it altogether, but how well you manage the suffering and your mental reaction to it are certainly things that you have a lot of control over.

Managing the Pain

A great place to start with managing the normal pain that comes from running hard is to see it for what it really is. We feel pain or fatigue and immediately interpret it as a bad sign. We think something is going wrong. We tell ourselves, "I shouldn't be hurting. I didn't train well enough. I'm running a bad race." In fact, feeling the pain, strain, and fatigue when you're exerting yourself is entirely natural. It is a good thing. You feel the way you do because you're giving it your best effort. You are pushing yourself to excel and to reach your maximum potential. You're striving to reach a goal that is not easily achieved. If you didn't feel that way, chances are you are underperforming or setting goals that don't reflect your true potential. Remember the first part of the anonymous saying, "Pain is inevitable…"

Realizing that the pain and strain you feel is normal and natural is important because it helps you avoid the other route your thinking might take, the negative route, which is to be overcome by fear and self-doubt. "If I feel this badly now, how much worse am I going to feel later?" you ask yourself. "I can just barely maintain this pace. How can I possibly keep this up for the rest of the race?" Thinking like that you quickly convince yourself that continuing to try is pointless, that the only solution is to train harder and try again next year, that your goal for now is out of reach. But you are never going to train your way out of feeling slammed when you are pushing yourself to your limits. Instead of continuing, you panic and give up.

When, on the other hand, you interpret the pain as a natural consequence of giving your best effort, you are in a position to keep the thinking positive and to employ mental strategies that will help you deal with the pain rather than give in to it. You want to be able to accept the pain, move beyond it, and get the focus back on what you need to be doing to maintain your effort. There are several mental strategies you can try. You might go into some kind of routine to relax yourself muscle group by muscle group from the top of your head down to your toes. You might focus your thinking on a positive, reassuring mantra. You might break down the race ahead of you into shorter, manageable segments. You might narrow your focus down to just the sensations you are experiencing in the present: the look of the road ahead of you, the sound of your footsteps, the feel of the air on your skin, your breathing, the motion of your arms. All of these actions pull the mind back away from the negative self-talk and help you stay positive and engaged with the task at hand.

One way to deal with the pain post race *© Rob Mann*

Of course, in theory all that sounds great. It's easy to imagine that you can just sidestep the negative thinking, not get discouraged, and soldier on as if you didn't feel like death warmed over. Tra-la-la. The reality is, though, that when you are in the actual situation, it is extremely difficult to not falter. Training helps. You get better at dealing with the pain and fatigue the more times you face difficult situations and have to cope with them. That is why pushing yourself hard from time to time during your workouts is a good idea. You get the physical benefits of training hard but you also are giving yourself invaluable practice at dealing with the mental aspects of being at your outer limits.

The up side of this dynamic is that if you succeed in not faltering, you have earned the self-satisfaction and pride that you feel from triumphing over a difficult situation. In other words, it is "To the stars *through difficulty*." The great thing about running is that it affords you this opportunity, this chance for growth, over and over again.

Interval Training

One excellent form of training to experience the dynamic of pushing yourself to the limit and then having to rely on your mind to keep yourself going is interval training. Interval training workouts involve alternating short bursts of very intense activity with periods of rest. There is nothing like interval training for making rapid gains in your ability to run faster. It raises your VO2 max level, which is a combination of the amount of oxygen-rich blood your heart can pump and your muscles' ability to use the oxygen. Interval training also burns calories like you were feeding coal into a raging furnace.

Doing 10K races was definitely the popular thing to do in the 1980s when I first started entering local races as part of my running routine. When I raced, I gave it everything I had. I always went for a PR and at first I saw my times dropping rapidly. Doing well at the race would spur me on to train harder and again I'd see progress in my finish times. Then I got to that point of diminishing returns where I'd really cashed in all the easy gains in my fitness. After that I needed to ramp up my training considerably to be able to run a PR.

Of course, I was familiar with interval training from my cross-country days. I knew what a nasty piece of work it was, but at the same time I also knew that if I wanted to keep lowering my 10K times, it would be the most efficient means to get there. I started going to the track a couple of times a week for my daily workout. Eventually my goal became breaking 40 minutes for the 10K, which required that I run the 6.1 miles at an average pace of 6 minutes and 25 seconds per mile. Elite runners and those who finish in the top five or ten percent of 10K races will laugh at these numbers, but for a middle-aged weekend warrior like me, these were tough goals.

My typical interval workout would be a one-mile warm-up circling the track at a jog. Then I would do a series of 6 or 8 half-mile intervals with a quarter mile easy jog between half miles and then a final one-mile jog around the track as a cool down. Given that I needed to be able to run six consecutive miles at roughly 6:30, my half-mile splits in the interval workouts needed to be at least under 3 minutes and 15 seconds. I could just barely do that. Mostly, my splits hovered around the 3:10 mark. Occasionally, I would reel off a split of 3:03 or 3:04, but never any faster. In other words, a 40-minute 10K was a very high goal for me. It meant running at pretty much my top sustainable speed throughout the race with no room for error.

The interval training sessions were always the highlight of my training week both physically and mentally. With every half-mile split, I would launch myself immediately up to race pace and hold it there as my body quickly went into an uncomfortable anaerobic zone. I'd get back to an aerobic zone as I jogged between the half-mile splits, but as soon as I launched back into race pace, I'd feel the burn of the anaerobic running. Of course, this dynamic is what raises your VO2 max level which makes interval training such an effective way to improve, but physically there is nothing there to really love.

Reaching for the stars one step at a time

Meanwhile, on the mental side, it was all fireworks. It took determination just to jump in the car and drive over to the track for the interval workouts knowing what was in store. The last half of each half-mile split was an exercise in patience as I clinched my teeth and held on to the best pace I could handle. The last two splits were always a final test of my determination to dig as deep as possible to hold the line on the pace, keep the time for those splits in line with the first four or five split times, and not blow up at the end. The intense struggle—both physical and mental—to get through the intervals made them my "to the stars through difficulty" moments. Afterwards, I would feel a charge of self-confidence and a sense that I was equal to any challenge.

To really get a sense of the mental turmoil and trauma that interval training can visit upon a runner, have a look at chapter 32 of John L. Parker, Jr.'s incredible running novel, *Once a Runner*. The chapter is appropriately titled "The Interval Workout," and it chronicles how the protagonist Quenton Cassidy is led through a series of intervals by his coach and fellow elite runner Bruce Denton. Cassidy completes a series of 20 quarter-mile repetitions with the understanding that this set of repeats is the bulk of the workout for the day. He views it as a solid workout, not easy but then not as demanding as he had expected. Denton then surprises him with the task of repeating the whole series, 20 more quarter miles, each at a very demanding pace. Cassidy bears down and manages 20 more quarters but at the end he is spent. The sun has gone down; no one is saying anything except to call out the number of the repetitions. Denton, who has been running alongside Cassidy up to this point, then leaves and promises to return when Cassidy has finished yet another surprise 20 quarter-mile repeats by himself. The description of Cassidy's mental state over those last 20 quarter miles is priceless and is a classic tale of how the mind must take up the fight when the body has seemingly been pushed beyond all limits.

I never did break 40 minutes in the 10K but the struggle I went through in trying was all to the good. I felt like I had reached the stars through difficulty. They didn't happen to be the sub-40 minute 10K stars I was aiming for. Instead, they were more like the despite-all-the-difficulties-you-did-your-very-best stars, but they were stars nonetheless.

Chapter 7

Jogging Club

Let's take a break from the heavy exposition here for a moment with a story. It picks up on a theme from the last chapter. I think we take for granted that the process of "reaching for the stars," that is, trying to better ourselves, to live a more satisfying life, entails struggle and work and overcoming challenges. Here's a story set in the future which imagines a time in which the challenge part of the process has been taken out of the equation.

Jogging Club

Lucjan found pumping his knees violently up and down completely unnatural, but he had to admit, it worked. He wasn't sure what to do with his arms. Hold them down by his sides? Bent up to his chest? He glanced at the other club members working their way around the edge of the large room.

Royan certainly looked the fool, barely lifting his feet off the floor, hands flopping at his waist. The others were the same, all pale as ghosts, their thin frames bent forward, their skinny legs and arms thrusting ahead.

It was Donall who had found the room for the meeting this week. The code came over Lucjan's receptor just the day before. It was the usual, an empty warehouse in an abandoned industrial sector. Work space was being concentrated several subfloors down nowadays. The robos were perfectly happy down there.

Once used to the strange motion, Lucjan began to savor the elaborate sensations. He felt the air whispering past his ears. He felt a strange warming in his thigh muscles. He checked his chrono. He'd been jogging for nearly four minutes. Many club members had already stopped at the water table, totally spent.

A spot of dampness was forming on his shirt. He was puzzling over that when the door at the far end of the warehouse burst open. Lucjan froze in horror. Several men in white uniforms poured in and fanned out. Even from the far end of the room, Lucjan could make out the large red hearts on their uniforms, agents of the Health Ministry.

The agents dropped quickly to one knee and assumed firing positions. Lucjan heard the pops of the guns going off and saw the gossamer nets explode out over one jogger after another.

By sheer luck, none of the agents had targeted him with their first shots. It gave him just enough time to recover himself and step through a nearby door. He pulled the door shut and heard a net slap against the other side.

Only a week before, the jogging club meeting had ended without incident. Tired and happy, he had slipped quietly back into his home unit. But his wife Mira had appeared at once, stepping out of their pharm closet to confront him.

"You're flushed," she said triumphantly.

"Just from the walk over from the tube," Lucjan replied.

She came closer, reached out and clamped her fingers around his thigh. It made him jump. "Your muscles are tight again. Don't you lie to me. You've been to that club."

Lucjan pushed past her and went into the bath area to look in the mirror. Sure enough, there was an unmistakable pink glow to his cheeks.

Mira was right behind him. "How can you do this to me?" she was saying. "Throwing your life away. For what?"

"It's just..." Lucjan began, "it's just...I don't know. I can't explain it. Jogging just makes you glad to be alive."

"Glad to be alive?" Mira shot back. "That's funny, when it's killing you. You know how it works. You can't fool the pill, Lucjan."

In his heart, he knew she was right. The longevity capsules kept you going an extra fifty years or so but only if you lived carefully, never stressing your body, never pushing your cells to work too hard. It was the best scientists could do. The aging process could be slowed, not stopped. People learned to adjust. It wasn't hard with robos doing all the work. Of course, sports were out. Before long, the government stepped in. People couldn't be trusted to look after themselves, so the Health Ministry was formed to enforce the regimen.

"What'll I do when you're gone?" Mira was saying. "All alone. No husband. No family."

"Stars above, Mira. What do you and I do now? What difference does it make if we do nothing for fifty more years?"

Mira looked at him and shook her head. "You're a fool," she said. "They'll catch you one of these days and put a stop to this."

She went over to her recliner and flopped down. "View," she whispered. The wall opposite her disappeared and the cast from Mira's favorite program appeared.

Lucjan stepped into the pharm closet where his evening tablets and longevity capsules were waiting in a plastic scoop. He popped them in his mouth and felt a tiny fizz as they dissolved instantly.

He walked back out and said goodnight to Mira. She ignored him. He stood behind her for a moment and watched a bit of the program.

"Gather round everybody," one of the actor's was saying, "Time to give great-great-grandpa his birthday certificate. One hundred and fifty sure is nifty!"

A large group of family members huddled around an ancient looking man reclining in an overstuffed motorized wheelchair. He

A future world where exercise is a thing of the past

was nearly pure white. His bony hand lifted unsteadily to accept the certificate.

Just then a tone sounded and everyone in the program turned to watch as the front door slid open. A Health Ministry official strode into the room with a stern look on his face.

“Come to congratulate grandpa on his birthday?” a woman who seemed to be the hostess asked.

“Afraid not, ma’am. Looking for a young man at this address, seen hurrying home from the tube this afternoon.” Everyone gasped. A boy of about sixteen was ushered forward, head down and hands in his pockets.

“Well, son,” said the official. “What did they teach you in school?”

"'Cause yourself pain, long life down the drain,'" the boy repeated obediently.

"That's right. You've got to form the habit of non-exertion early. You want to live to see one hundred and fifty like this fellow, don't you?"

"Sure," the boy said, glancing over at the guest of honor.

The official patted the boy on the shoulder and coaxed a smile out of him. "I believe we're okay here," he said to the hostess. "Enjoy your party now." The door slid to behind him as he left.

Lucjan sighed and kissed his wife on the top of her head.

He went over to his sleeping area and rolled onto his sleeper. He thought about that day's club meeting. Royan had brought an old sports tape. It showed a man jogging barefoot, running outdoors down an ancient street. Water poured off of the man. His lips trembled but his head was very steady. His legs and arms were skinny but his muscles were well developed. He jogged on and on and on. It was like he would never grow tired.

"I bet he was dead the next day," Donall had said. "Using himself up like that."

"I don't know," countered Royan. "There was a time when people thought it was good to jog like that. They thought the stronger you got, the better."

Everyone laughed at that.

“Yeah, Royan,” Donall said. “And raw food beats pharms, too. Right?”

Lucjan turned on his sleeper trying to get comfortable. But he couldn’t get the man’s face out of his mind.

Escape Plans

Lucjan had no idea which way to flee down the hallway to escape from the Health Ministry agents. He picked one way at random and hurried off. Left turn, right turn. He trotted down one dimly lit passageway after another. Eventually, he stumbled onto a tube stop. A handful of people were waiting there. A couple of them glanced in his direction, but there was no sign of any agents. Lucjan decided his luck had held.

A tube car glided to a stop in front of him. He swung inside and took a seat. As the car sped up, a faint tone sounded in Lucjan’s ear, a reminder to signify his destination. He pressed his home station icon on the panel. As he slumped back into his seat, the gravity of what had happened began to sink in. His club friends would be confined and monitored. Drugs would be used to adjust their attitudes. They would never dream of jogging again.

But even more ominous, the Health Ministry would know about him as well. Someone would reveal his name. Lucjan sat up with a start. They could be on their way to his unit right now! They’d be waiting for him! He had to think—and fast. Then he remembered that Royan had warned him about this possibility when he first joined the club.

“It’s already in your receptor,” he had said, “in case we’re found out. Just enter the code. It’s…”

My stars! Lucjan thought. What was the code? He tried to remain calm. He fumbled in his pocket for the receptor and glanced at the tube map to check his location. Still three stops before he changed tubes. Mercifully, it came to him. “Fixx,” he whispered into the receptor. “F…I…X…X.”

A sector and building number came up on the receptor’s tiny screen. Lucjan felt relief mixed with apprehension. He knew where he could go now, but what would he find there? And what about Mira? Just being able to go home to her suddenly seemed like such a wonderful thing. Her warning rang in his ear. Maybe she was right. The stupid jogging club was going to cost him everything.

A soft voice issued from the headrest of Lucjan’s seat. “Please change to tube F-3 at the next stop for your destination,” it said.

Lucjan double-checked the sector number on his receptor and then pressed a new destination on the panel. The voice issued updated instructions, “Please remain on this tube at the next stop. You will change at tube V-35.” The car pulled into the stop where Lucjan would have changed to go home. He watched the distinctive patterns on the walls slide away as he continued on. An icy chill rode up his spine as the last of the familiar stop blinked away.

The sector was on the outskirts of the metropolis where Lucjan lived, near one of the abandoned regions. He emerged from the tube stop blinking into the sunlight. There was not even a protective covering built over the streets here. Dire warnings about direct exposure of the skin to the sun crowded Lucjan's mind. He was so distracted he could barely follow the building numbers as the sidewalk transporter whisked him along.

Finally, he spotted the correct number and stepped off the transporter. The building was a huge dilapidated warehouse. Oddly, the large façade had but a single normal-sized doorway for entry. Finding no buttons or panels, Lucjan knocked on the faded wood of the door.

"Come on in," he heard someone call.

He stepped into a tiny room that offered only ancient peeling wallpaper and a bland-looking man sitting behind a desk. The man said nothing, just looked at Lucjan inquisitively.

A future world where jogging is forbidden

"I…I was in a club," Lucjan stammered out, "a jogging club. Some agents from the Health Ministry burst in…but I got away. I haven't been home at all." Lucjan spread his hands plaintively. "I've come here with nothing."

For a long while, the man didn't speak. He just stared. Finally, he asked, "What's the code?"

"Fixx. F…I…X…X."

"Who gave you that?"

"Royan Krel. He was the head of my club. I think the agents got him with the others."

"And you are…?"

"Lucjan Ginn." And then, needlessly, Lucjan added, "My wife is Mira Ginn."

The man drew a slim reader from a drawer, thumbed a button, and checked the screen. Apparently satisfied, he said, "Right through there, sir," as he pressed something underneath the desk. The wall next to Lucjan slid apart along a hidden seam revealing another door. The door opened with a gentle whoosh revealing a vast inner space flooded with light. Lucjan stepped inside and had to catch his breath at what he saw. Well below where he stood was a vast oval track. Bright white lines ran along it marking off lanes. Maybe a hundred joggers were there either striding resolutely around the brick red track or stretched out on a bright green infield resting and chatting. A few of the runners on the track moved with the clumsy, uneven gait familiar to Lucjan from his club meetings, but other runners glided along the track with a sleek grace reminiscent of the runner he had seen in the tape.

"Rather impressive, don't you think?" A small man with a scraggly white goatee had appeared at Lucjan's elbow. He was dressed in a costume Lucjan recognized as an ancient sweatsuit. The man's pointy Adam's apple bobbed up and down under the leathery skin of his neck as he spoke. "We'll have you down there in no time after we get you settled."

"What is this place?"

"Ah, yes. Our little subterfuge, the falling-down warehouse. Well, we couldn't stay hidden long if we covered all this over with a big shiny dome, now could we?"

"But who are you…who are all these people?"

The man chuckled. "Who are we? I'll tell you who we are. We're you. We're all the people like you that are fed up with the Health Ministry running our lives, keeping us weak, feeding us poison. You were part of one of our little farm team enterprises. We have many out there, you know, all over this metropolis and the other cities. We're training for the day that we can rise up and take our lives back."

Just then there was a commotion below them on the track. An older runner, a man Lucjan judged to be about his age, had been running strongly but then suddenly began weaving. Lucjan watched in horror as the man clutched his chest and grimaced. A second later the man slammed clumsily down onto the track surface and went motionless.

Two attendants popped out onto the track, one pushing a gurney. They bent over the man for a moment, then lifted the limp body onto the gurney and covered it with a white sheet. As they slowly wheeled the gurney away, several runners had to break stride to let them pass, but otherwise the activity down below went on just as before.

"What in the stars?" Lucjan exclaimed looking to the man beside him.

The man calmly pulled at his goatee, as if lost in thought. "Come this way," he said, taking Lucjan's arm. "Perhaps we should visit the shrine now. It will help you understand."

They crossed over to a set of double doors that swung open when the man waved his hand over a sensor. The room within was filled with dim blue light. The ceiling was formed by a series of arches. Sleek aluminum benches marched up to what appeared to be an altar. On the wall behind the altar was an enormous picture of a somewhat stocky man with longish wavy hair dressed in running shorts and a sweatshirt with white piping running down each sleeve. The man was in full stride coming directly at the camera, his forward thrusting leg bulging with muscle, his hands hanging relaxed by his side.

"Our patron saint, our scholar," the man said, "and our first martyr, Mr. James Fixx. You see he devoted himself to running, lived his life for it. Wrote our bible. Come. Have a look."

They approached the altar and there under a sturdy glass case lit from below lay an object that Lucjan at first didn't recognize. It was rectangular and the top of it had faded to a light pink.

There were white letters running across the top that were barely discernible. Lucjan struggled to make them out. "The… Complete…Book…" he said out loud. Of course, it was a book. There were still books around when Lucjan was a boy but it had been so long ago. "The Complete Book…of Running."

"We think this is the only copy still in existence. It is very old, very precious."

"You said he was a martyr?"

"Yes. You see running had given him everything. It had restored him and remade him. He ran every day and caused great numbers of others to run also. They called it 'the running boom.' But the doctors discovered that his heart was not sound and told him to stop, that running would kill him. But he wouldn't stop. He chose running over life, or rather I should say he chose running as life. Of course, the doctors were right. They found him one day on the side of a road. His heart had failed just as they predicted."

"What a shame."

"A shame? No, not at all. It was what he chose of his own free will. And now he shows us the way back to life from the living death that the Health Ministry hands us and only calls life. All of us here have chosen to follow his lead. We gladly give up our long pointless lives to find something in ourselves—if only for a moment—worth living for. But you already know this. Why else did you come to one of our clubs?"

"But what about that man down there on the track. Why did he collapse?"

"To be one of us, you must first give up the pills. They keep you weak. You can't develop as a runner as long as you take that poison. Unfortunately, without the pills, the aging process advances quickly and...well, you saw the result. How old are you now?"

"One hundred and ten," Lucjan said.

"So on pharms, you would last another forty years or so. Here you might last ten, fifteen at most."

Lucjan swallowed hard.

"It's your decision. If you choose to go home, you are free to go. You'll need a simple procedure to blank us from your memory. It is painless and harmless. Or you can stay with us and embrace life. It is up to you."

Lucjan chose to stay but he only lasted one week. His stomach never felt right as he tried to adjust to the fruits and vegetables that replaced his pharms. At night, he tossed and turned on his probeless mattress. The soreness in his muscles was a constant torment. His excitement to get out on the track quickly turned to dread as he learned that progress only came from pushing himself hard, well beyond his comfort level. The other runners reminded him over and over, "No pain, no gain," until he was ready to scream. Years of indolence had left not only his muscles slack but his mind and his will as well.

And he missed Mira. He had trouble remembering what had been so wrong about lounging around the unit with her all day, watching her programs, chatting with her about the neighbors in the unit next door. How could he throw away so many years with her—just to run?

After a week, Lucjan sought out the man with the white goatee. "Give me the memory procedure," he said. "I want to go home."

Home

A few months later, Mira and Lucjan were sharing a recliner, enjoying Mira's favorite show, when suddenly the scene before them dissolved and a pulsating red light introducing a special news report appeared. A newscaster materialized before them superimposed over a live scene unfolding behind her.

"…the discovery of a large dissident group here in the V sector…" she was saying.

Behind her, two Health Ministry agents were struggling with a man on the ground who was trying to free himself from a net. One of the agents had his knee on the man's neck, forcing his head down, and grinding the man's chin with its white goatee into the ground. Still the man kicked and struggled.

The sound from the scene was just audible below the louder voice of the newscaster. The man could be heard crying out, "'We are reasserting…our kinship with ancient man, and even with the wild beasts that preceded him. This…is our secret, one we share every time we go running.' The words of James Fixx, you fools! Hear me, fools, hear me!" The agent stuck a needle into the man's neck and he went still.

Lucjan shook his head. “My stars, what a fanatic,” he said to Mira. “That’s it for me. I’m going to bed.” Lucjan rose and left Mira to the news broadcast. She watched the agent dragging the man away. For some reason, she thought back to when Lucjan had disappeared for a whole week and then just showed up one morning all dazed and confused. She was sure it had something to do with that awful club he used to go to, but he had sworn up and down he didn’t know what she was talking about.

Meanwhile, Lucjan finished up in the bath area and then rolled onto his sleeper. The probes floated up to do their work, gently nudging the few tight spots in Lucjan’s shoulders and back. Lucjan sighed deeply. He turned over on his side and drifted off to sleep, not a thought in his head.

Chapter 8

No Man Is an Island

Running is an individual sport. You may benefit from a great support team. There may be a circle of fellow runners from your club cheering you on. The marathon you're running may be littered with great aid stations and a thousand pumped-up volunteers. There may be a huge infrastructure behind you, giving you your chance at a PR, but in the end, it is you who manages every step and you alone who guts out that last mile to the finish line. No one can do your running for you. It's just the nature of running that your achievements are your own, and this is no doubt part of the reason running is such a fountain of self-esteem and self-satisfaction.

But often it is something from outside yourself that provides that final spark when it seems like you've exhausted all your mental and physical resources and you're convinced that throwing in the towel is the only option. Have you ever gotten to the final quarter mile of a 5K or 10K, convinced that you gave it everything you had, certain that you couldn't quicken your pace even if a bear were chasing you, only to discover the runner who you have been trying to beat for years is just ahead of you? Suddenly you find another gear.

Or have you been in the death throes of the final mile of a marathon, feeling the full weight of the last three hours of killing yourself, and then you look over and see a little kid matching you stride for stride? Now, more power to the kid who might be the greatest running prodigy since Mercury, but somehow you find yourself capable of picking up the pace just enough to ensure that your name will not appear in the final results listed just below 13-year-old Sparky Sparkolino.

Try With a Little Help From Your Friends

There are many ways to leverage the strength of fellow runners when you're training or racing, both when you desperately need a boost and when you're just looking to shift the attention away from your own private running hell for a while. It's easy to get so inwardly focused when running and so absolutely reliant on what you are doing and feeling that you miss the possibility that others might be able to step in and provide just the help you need.

I experienced a classic example of being helped along my way once at the Rio Del Lago 100-Mile Run several years ago. It took the extreme of a 100-mile race to create this clarifying moment for me, but the lesson can apply to any running situation. This year I was running the race all alone. It was early Sunday morning, still dark, when I got to an aid station at about the 80-mile mark. I was very tired and hurting when I flopped down on a camp chair and began preparing my hydration pack for the next section of trail. It so happened that the course looped back and forth on itself, and I was at a point where the actual finish was only five miles away. To continue, though, I had to head away from the finish before eventually coming back to where I was sitting. I couldn't get the nearness of that finish line out of my mind.

Exhaustion washed over me and suddenly the whole struggle just felt like more than I could endure. I glanced behind me and saw that the aid station was set up next to a big parking lot with crowds of volunteers and people supporting runners coming and going even though it was the middle of the night. Getting a ride back to my car at the start/finish would be so easy, I realized, and my hotel was just a five-minute drive away from there. I could literally go from this chair and the torture of this race to a warm, comfy bed in less than fifteen minutes. The impulse to act on that thought was overwhelming.

Talk to Paul

Just then a volunteer saw me sitting there and came over. "How ya doin'?" she asked. "Can I get you anything?"

"Actually," I said, "I'm thinking of dropping."

She glanced at her watch, gave me a long stare, and then said, "You need to talk to Paul."

"Fine," I said, "but I can get a ride to the start/finish from here, right?"

"Talk to Paul," she said and disappeared.

I sat there motionless, head drooping, thinking through my decision to quit. My resolve had crumbled. I could think of no good reason to keep going. What did it matter? I'd even finished this race before so what was the big deal if I didn't make it this time? Who would care? It wasn't worth it. There was always a next time.

Then Paul approached. He was a middle-aged guy with a neatly trimmed beard, wearing a hoodie and a baseball cap. He crouched down in front of me. He was lean and moved easily, like being up all night working an aid station was nothing for him. He was obviously a runner. He looked at me for a while.

Finally, he spoke, "I know just how you feel. I've been there myself, a million times."

That was all he said, but it was like Luke Skywalker had launched his proton torpedoes into the depths of the Death Star. His words burrowed into my mind, neatly evading all the opposing flak, worming through the narrow tunnels, and then exploding with fire and light at the heart of my dark thinking. I was not alone. I shared my agony with Paul, who had borne this burden in the past. I shared it with all the other runners who were stumbling through the night around me. WE felt awful, not just me. WE wanted to quit, not just me.

"Just relax," Paul went on. "Give yourself ten minutes. Sip some ice water. Then get up and start walking down the trail. You've got plenty of time. Just keep going. It's worked for me."

I followed his advice and was soon hiking back up the trail in the dark away from the finish. My only goal was the next aid station and then I figured I could re-evaluate things. But it never came to that. I marched through the last 20 miles of the race without a moment's doubt that I was good to make it to the end. It had just been that one weak moment when the idea of the closeness of the finish line had run riot over all my defenses against giving up. But Paul had set me right with his simple, heartfelt message. He understood my suffering and felt like it was something I could overcome. That's all I needed to hear.

Using other runners to direct your mind away from your own insular thinking will often help you get back into a positive frame of mind. When you realize your self-talk has turned negative or you're clearly pushing through a "valley," start talking to the runners around you. Just the distraction of trying to relate to another human being will usually crowd out thoughts about yourself and how you feel. Plus, as soon as you get into a conversation with someone, you get this sense that things can't be that bad. After all, you can still act normal and relate to someone else even if you feel like hell. The conversation will also lead you into thinking about things other than how you feel. As long as you're concentrating on telling a joke, or listening to the other runner's story, or filling each other in on your running backgrounds, you are making progress in the race without letting the negative thoughts undermine you.

If you don't feel like talking, you can still form an attachment with another runner without saying anything. Just focus on the

A train of runners can pull you along when you're feeling tired.

runner and follow along. Pretend that person is pulling you forward or pulling you up a hill. Get into a line of runners and just concentrate on the runner's feet in front of you. Fall into the same rhythm with everybody else, relax, and imagine that the train of runners is helping you move along.

I was once in a marathon when a big headwind sprang up and it suddenly felt about twice as hard to maintain the race pace I was shooting for. I started drafting off other runners. I'd jump from one runner to another if my chosen runner wasn't moving fast enough. Of course, drafting off of strangers was uncool, but I tried to leave enough distance between myself and the runner I was following so as not to be annoying. At any rate, I spent so much time focusing on drafting, keeping up with people, and planning my jumps from one runner to another that those hard miles in the wind went by quickly.

One year at the San Francisco Marathon, I ran with my friend Mike, an army captain, who had moved into a house on my block and had become my training partner. He was wearing a t-shirt with a big, red, impossible-to-miss Canadian maple leaf on the front. From time to time, actually almost continuously, as we ran along people were shouting at us, "Canada! Canada!" Mike would wave graciously and nod his head in acknowledgement. This went on the whole race. When we reached the crowds at the finish line, it was like every other person there was from Canada, there was such a major uproar when Mike crossed the line.

Of course, I was happy as could be. All the hoopla was wonderfully distracting. I'd sort of floated along in Mike's Canada-inspired bubble, hardly focusing on the fact that I was running a marathon at all. I turned to Mike as we were walking to the food tent with our finisher's medals around our necks, clutching our space blankets over our shoulders, and said, "Were you born in Canada or something? I didn't even know you were from there."

"I'm not," he said.

"You lived there?"

"Nope," he said.

"You have nothing to do with Canada?" I asked.

"Nope, nothing, I just wear the shirt," he said, smiling.

At another marathon, the California International Marathon in Sacramento, I just happened to be running at about the same pace as a guy wearing a "Praise Jesus!" t-shirt. He seemed like a real character with a long beard and a thick moustache. He had an Oakland Raiders cap jammed down over long wavy hair that hung halfway down his back. His shirt was drawing comments from bystanders. "Amen!" people would shout or "God bless." Every time someone said something he would light up and yell back, "Praise the Lord and pass the ammunition!"

This went on and on. "Jesus loves!"

"Praise the Lord and pass the ammunition."

"Run for Jesus!"

"Praise the Lord and pass the ammunition."

I felt like I'd wandered into a marathon Christian revival meeting. I couldn't help but adjust my pace a little bit here and there so that I kept the guy close by. I wondered how long he could keep it up, and how long his enthusiasm would last before the hard running took its toll. As it turns out, he never wavered. He got to the finish still waving and shouting, "Praise the Lord and pass the ammunition." Maybe Jesus was sustaining him. I know the guy was certainly sustaining me. Watching him kept me totally occupied through the last hard six miles of the race.

Just overhearing remarks made by other runners can be diverting. Once again, I was in San Francisco running the marathon when I heard someone behind me saying, "Listen to your body. Just listen to your body." I slowed a bit and a couple passed me. It was a neatly appointed guy in a silky, coordinated running outfit next to a woman who was obviously struggling. The guy was clearly running well within his comfort zone. He had no trouble jogging along and talking constantly, dispensing advice to the woman. For her part, she looked about ready to collapse. “Listen to your body,” he kept saying, which seemed to be his entire coaching strategy. I’m sure her body was quite vocally telling her that it was about to die, and I’m also sure that what she wanted more than anything else was for her running buddy to shut up so she wouldn’t have to listen to him.

I sped up to get away from this unhappy duo, but soon encountered a young guy with a big bushy head of curly blonde hair who was breezing along and telling everybody around him, “Hey, I’m a running machine, baby, a real running machine.” We were at about the halfway point in the marathon. I was not too experienced with marathons at the time, but I knew enough to guess that the running machine man might have a different perspective on events later in the race. He went on by and disappeared up ahead. Sure enough, about five miles later, I spotted his distinctive hair in the crowd. He was walking on a slightly uphill section through Chinatown. His head was down and he looked pretty done in. He was no longer letting everybody around him know what a running machine he was. Contemplating his plight kept me occupied for the next several miles right when I might have slipped into death march mode myself.

Now I’m not dispensing any specific strategies here. I’m not telling you to wear a Canadian t-shirt or find religion or spend all your time eavesdropping on other runners. What I’m saying is that if you shift your focus to the people around you, it might well open up a little mental space for you to occupy when you might otherwise be struggling. I even make it a point to talk to

I even talk to all the dogs I meet along the way to occupy my mind.

all the dogs I meet along the way when I'm out for a run. I tell each dog what a good dog it is. And for just a little while I'm in a good place, thinking about dogs and how great they are rather than thinking about running and how tired I feel.

Night in the Mark Twain National Forest

My experience at Rio Del Lago certainly taught me that you can fall deep into a mental sinkhole but still make it back out if you stay open to some help from outside. My ultimate experience along those lines came in another 100-mile run, also deep in the night, this time in the Mark Twain National Forest in south central Missouri at the Ozark Trail 100-Mile Endurance Run. I was with my long-time running buddy, Rob Mann, and as we were running along through the dark forest, I realized that I had "gone dark."

On paper, the Ozark 100 didn't appear to be such a formidable challenge beyond the fact that it was a hundred miles long. The forested terrain was rolling but the elevation change was not dramatic. There were no mountains and no steep rocky climbs. This was central Missouri, not western Colorado. The early November race date promised no high temps and no brutal sun. And yet the race harbored a few notable surprises.

Foremost was that the entire one hundred and two miles of single-track trail was covered in about three inches of dead leaves that obscured the many rocks, ruts, and roots that formed a constant tripping hazard for almost the whole race. It didn't take long to learn that you had to adapt to the trail by slowing down, spreading your feet wider than normal, running a little more upright than usual, and sort of probing forward with a flat foot strike for almost every step of the way. The closer you got to imitating a running duck, the better, but you were still tripping and falling all the time no matter what you did.

The race began in five o'clock darkness at a rather non-descript trailhead on a non-descript country road. The forest closed in around us as soon as we started running. There was nothing out there except trees for most of the way. Civilization was not very evident along the entire course. After running all day, a pitch-black darkness descended at six pm and didn't let up for the next thirteen hours. You felt lost in the midst of nowhere. It was like the light had left the world and was never coming back. From time to time, you'd pop out of the forest onto a deserted stretch of blacktop or an empty jeep road, but that would only serve to highlight the loneliness. Then you'd be back in the forest. There was something of a Blair Witch quality to following the trail at night. Shadows constantly jumped around you in a black and gray world. Myriad green spider eyes were shining up at you from the forest floor. With the trail hidden under the leaves, you had to guess which opening in the trees was your route.

The endless night was made worse by a section of the course where the aid stations were spaced far apart. Usually aid stations are placed every five or six miles which keeps the running time between stations to around an hour and a half. At the Ozark 100, the night section of the course included a stretch where the aid stations were back-to-back-to-back segments of 9 miles, 10 miles, and 8 miles. The 10-mile stretch late at night after running all day probably took us about three hours to cover, and this was staggering around out in the endless woods, tripping constantly on hidden rocks, feeling our way along a trail we couldn't see, and wondering all the while if we were lost. The three hours seemed like twice that measured in desperate, bleak mind time. We called this part of the course Murderer's Row.

By the time we were on the final eight-mile stretch of Murderer's Row heading for the Berryman Campground aid station, I was not in good shape. Normally when Rob and I run together, it is constant chatter. We go over running plans, play trivia games, exchange jokes, talk about politics, talk about family, curse and swear, get crazy, and trash talk each other until the cows come home. I can always tell we are in trouble when one of us "goes dark," that is, when the chatter stops, when the answers to questions become a single word, when one or the other of us is no longer loudly complaining but rather moving along totally silent, lost in a world of pain and suffering.

When Berryman Campground wouldn't come, I went dark and I could feel it. Hope died within me. The night wouldn't end. Everything hurt. Getting through the fucking leaves and running like a duck had just gotten to be too much. I didn't want to talk. I didn't want to keep fighting. I just wanted to have it all be over with. I was ready to quit but the thing that weighed on me most was not dragging Rob down with me. We had just had a bad experience back in California at the San Diego 100-Mile Run where we'd basically egged each other on into dropping because we didn't want to face a little rain and cold.

Actually, an unusual thing had happened in San Diego. At the aid station where things looked very bleak, we ran into a volunteer who was totally okay with the idea that we wanted to quit. "What's up ahead?" we'd asked, eyeing a steep uphill jeep road that was the next segment of the course and which was fast turning into mud in a light rain.

"It's a BIG hill," the volunteer had said ominously. "A couple of very good runners just came back down and dropped. They said the weather up there was awful." We paused and looked at each other. "It's the longest climb in the whole race," the volunteer added unhelpfully.

I had put on all the clothes I had with me and I was still shivering. Rob looked like a drowned rat and couldn't seem to get himself to look at the steep road we would have to climb.

The volunteer perked up. “We’ve got a nice warm camper here. You boys can climb right in. A couple of other runners are already in there.”

The Moment of Truth

The moment had come. I figured if we got into that camper we were never coming back out. Inertia was going to pin us in there. All desire to fight on was going to melt in the warm comfort of sitting down in a heated place and giving in to the exhaustion. I’m not even sure which one of us said it, but someone said, “Let’s quit. I’ve had it.” And then either I agreed with Rob or Rob agreed with me. The volunteer ripped open the door to the camper and sealed our fate.

Neither of us has ever doubted for even a second that it was one of the most boneheaded decisions we’d ever made in our running careers. Not surprisingly, the other runners in the campers were of no help. They both looked like they’d had encounters with speeding Mack trucks. One lay crumpled up on the camper’s bed, totally motionless, perhaps dead. The other was leaning out of a chair, head down, arm hooked around a post, ready to tumble on the floor, also perhaps dead.

Rob and I sat looking at each other. For two minutes, it seemed like we’d done the right thing. The warm camper was heaven. The race had just been too much. We’d decided together to drop. It wasn’t like I’d wimped out by myself. I had company. However, it didn’t take long before I started feeling much better. If we’d gotten into the camper with the notion that we would warm up and then get back on the trail, I think it would have worked out just fine. But we'd burned all our bridges behind us. We'd told the volunteers we were done, asked for a ride to the finish, and let down all our mental defenses against quitting as soon as we'd shrugged off our hydration packs and dumped them on the floor of the camper.

So in Missouri, I wanted to get out of the race again but not pressure Rob to do the same. I had gone totally dark. I don't think I'd uttered a word for ten minutes. I'd been just mechanically trudging behind Rob on the single track trail, trying to stay upright, running like a duck, and sinking deeper and deeper into despair over ever reaching the next aid station. Finally, in the mousiest, little, tiny, trembling voice in the world, I said, "Rob, if I quit at Berryman, will you keep going?"

Rob didn't hesitate for even an instant. He turned around and yelled, "We're NOT quitting! You can FORGET that!"

I was stunned. I was deep in my pain cave thinking that the last of my resolve had been buried in the leaves, but this time Rob was in a totally different place. He'd learned the lesson of San Diego and was applying it here with a sledgehammer. If he hadn't sounded so certain, if there had been just a little crack in his resolve, I might have wavered, but as it was, he was like a spelunker that had been lowered into my pain cave and was handing me a lifeline back to the surface.

It kept me running and now I was at least thinking through the possibilities. "If I'm going on, I need to sleep at this next aid station," I said.

"That's fine. You can nap for a while and then we go on. NO quitting!"

Berryman Campground finally came and it was amazing. The volunteer there sat me down at an empty table, found my drop bag, and dumped the contents out on the table so I didn't even have to bend over to find my stuff. A down blanket appeared over my shoulders and soup and sandwiches were served like I was at a fine restaurant. Meanwhile, Rob was having some blisters expertly lanced, disinfected, and dressed. I took a fifteen-minute nap under the comforter, ate some more soup, and got my pack ready for the next leg. I was back from the brink and ready to go.

The first light was just breaking after the long night as we struck out on the trail. Soon our lights weren't necessary and the previously all-gray world took on hues of brown, orange, and yellow. With the dawn, I felt more energetic. It was the morning bump that you can usually count on after running all night, when your biological clock would normally be waking you up and getting you charged up for the new day. Rob had rescued me. His unexpected hard line on not even contemplating quitting had done the trick. Left to my own devices, I would have been through at Berryman Campground. With Rob's help, and with the great treatment at the aid station, I was able to keep going.

The only argument left for us to have that day happened when we got to the last mile. I wanted to walk it in and savor the finish. Rob wanted to run it in and finish strong. We compromised, walking for a while but then picking it up over the final quarter mile of open field. We each collected a finisher's belt buckle, but there was no doubt in my mind that I owed getting mine to Rob.

Chances are you've experienced going dark at some point in your running. The fun meter is all pegged out, the legs are dead, and your attitude is in the toilet. Keep in mind that in addition to the obvious two options, that is, quitting or pulling yourself out of your own funk, there is a third option. Someone might be around who can give you a helping hand. Be aware of that prospect and seek it out.

The long night of leaves and an endless dark forest

Chapter 9

My Heart Left Me in San Francisco

Market Street is San Francisco's main drag, a wide boulevard that cuts dramatically up through the city on a diagonal that makes a total hash out of the place. It's usually jammed with cars, buses, trolleys, pedestrians, homeless beggars, and gawking tourists. On one day in August of 1984, however, a long stretch of Market Street had been closed to traffic for the running of the San Francisco Marathon. I was there at the bottom of Market Street in the shadow of the imposing buildings of the Embarcadero Center, in the final mile of the race. It was my first ever marathon. There was a steady river of runners flowing up Market Street, and because of the rise in elevation, I could see all the way up to where the marathoners were turning off Market about a mile away to finish in front of City Hall.

People were cheering. The sun was out. The city was an alien, engulfing, unreal place. It was hard to believe I was even there, engaged in this amazing struggle to complete a marathon. It was the farthest I had ever run. I had started with no earthly idea as to what was going to happen that day. Now I was almost finished. To my surprise, more than half the runners ahead of me were walking. To their credit they were walking pretty fast, measuring out big strides uphill on the pavement, but walking none the less. They clearly would have preferred to be running, but apparently the twenty-five miles they'd traveled so far had beaten them into submission.

I did not have that problem. God knows I would have loved to give in and walk a stretch. Every muscle in my legs screamed with pain. I'd hit the wall several miles back, actually splattered up against the wall really hard, but I'd managed to tough that out and keep running. Strangely, the worst pains I felt were in the crooks of my elbows. I must have been holding my arms up too high against my chest the whole race without

The city by the bay

realizing it. I probably looked like a Tyrannosaurus Rex running down the street with my little forearms dangling in front of me.

On the plus side, making it to the last mile of my first marathon had charged me up with a massive load of adrenaline. I was passing the walkers like they were standing still. Being able to run at the end of this ordeal was magic. With all the training, all the anticipation, and all the nerves that I'd been through to get to this point now behind me, I felt like I was flying. In fact, I was having the quintessential big city marathon experience.

The San Francisco Marathon had been launched in 1977 when a thousand runners had come together to run a course that was mostly confined to Golden Gate Park with a loop around nearby Lake Merced, and a short stretch up and down the Great Highway overlooking the Pacific Ocean. It wasn't until 1982 that organizers managed to plot a course that toured the city.

The vision was to make San Francisco one of the premier marathons in the country and have it take its place alongside New York and Boston. It had the full support of then-Mayor Dianne Feinstein who wanted to showcase her city. It was Feinstein who green-lit taking the race beyond Golden Gate Park. San Francisco's unique weather allowed for the novelty of staging a big marathon in the middle of the summer. In 1983, the race became the first marathon in the USA to award every finisher a medal. By 1984, the race had grown to 7,000 competitors, so as I made my way up Market Street toward the finish, it felt exactly like what it was, a major, up-and-coming, citywide, top-flight marathon happening right in the sweet spot of the running boom.

We'd been through the Mission District, Golden Gate Park, Marina Green, and the Presidio with views of the Golden Gate Bridge. We'd run through Chinatown and the Haight-Ashbury neighborhood. We'd gone by Lombard Street and Fisherman's Wharf, and we'd looked out at Alcatraz. It was pavement all the way, very tough on the feet and legs, but there were always runners nearby to key off of and of course the distracting scenery of one of the world's most unique and beautiful cities. By the time I'd crossed the finish line, had a medal slipped over my head, a space blanket thrown over my shoulders, and collapsed on the grass in front of City Hall, I felt like I'd traveled through a whole lifetime. I understood from beginning to end the incredible allure of the marathon.

Of course, I wasn't alone. By 1984, tens of thousands of people were running marathons and the craze has only grown. Now hundreds of thousands finish the marathon distance every year worldwide. The achievement has become a signature bucket-list athletic goal pursued equally by people from all walks of life. It's worth considering just why the marathon has become such a widespread and iconic achievement.

I think the answer lies in the way preparing for and running a marathon takes you on such a profound and validating journey of self-discovery. First of all, nobody—with maybe a few exceptions—will go into marathon training with complete confidence that they are going to succeed. Experienced runners who have worked up to five miles appreciate how difficult it is to cover even that relatively modest distance. So now you're talking about running twenty-six miles in one go? Well, that seems inconceivable. It takes a leap of faith to even think that you're going to run that far.

Then there is the size of the challenge you are committing to and the time it will take. If you're starting from scratch, you are looking at probably at least six months of focused effort. Even if you've done enough running to have a solid base to work off of, you should plan on a three- or four-month training program to get fully prepared. Getting ready for a marathon is a big project. Regarding family and work, you will likely have to move some things around or forego some things in order to find the time to get all the running done, especially the critical time- and energy-consuming long weekend runs. Put that much effort into accomplishing anything, sacrificing things along the way, and you'll find you have an enormous stake in succeeding.

Once you're in the training cycle for the marathon, you will experience perhaps the single most remarkable part of your marathon training journey, which is extending your long runs every weekend or every other weekend to distances that seemed impossible to you before. Having believed that five miles stretched your limits, you will find your ten-mile weekend amazing. And by adding just one or two miles a week to your long run, you keep your advances manageable but still break new ground every week and set new personal records for distances run. As you get to the upper teens and advance toward a long run of twenty miles, you discover new things about yourself. You explore your capacity for suffering and for staying tough as the miles pile up. You learn the critical importance of your mental attitude. And of course you find out all about your physical self, what hurts, what breaks down, and what you need to eat and drink to keep yourself going.

With all the training behind you, the race date approaches and naturally the nerves ramp up. Traveling and staying overnight where the race is located may be complicated. The night before the race, you may struggle to sleep. On race morning, you have to eat, pull your gear together, and get to the race venue on time.

Finally, there is the race itself. The reality of the 26.2 miles is that it is a very long way and nobody is going to go the distance without finding some trouble along the way. You may be on schedule at the halfway point of the race and feeling confident, but by the late teen miles you will be suffering. Miles 20 through 25 are going to hurt like nothing else you have ever experienced in your life. Time will slow to a crawl. Whereas before you were ticking off the miles like they were nothing, now you will be searching the horizon for the next mile marker and it will never, ever come.

Your weekend training runs will take you down long, lonely roads, sometimes in less than ideal conditions.

You will run out of readily available energy and hit the wall, at which time you will struggle just to lift your arms and legs.

Staying on pace will become a mammoth effort. But it is because of this very struggle and the difficulty of the last six miles that you will be forced to encounter your true self, to find out, as they say, what you are made of. Running a marathon is not a team sport. As we've noted before, you alone do all the running. There is nowhere to hide and there are no get-out-of-jail-free cards. How you react to the pain and what you are able to accomplish is all on you. The corollary to that, though, is that whatever you do manage to do rebounds to your credit and your credit alone.

It is also liberating and exhilarating to actually be in the fight and to be responsible for your own destiny. You are not in any way a spectator when you're running a marathon. I always feel this deep gulf between myself and the bystanders along the marathon route as I stream by with the other runners. We runners are locked in a monumental struggle. We are engaging the beast. We have the blood and sweat and dirt on our faces. But we also have the potential for greatness, if we persevere and overcome the challenge and finish. The bystanders are just having another day. The runners are possibly having one of the best days of their lives.

The joy and relief and exhilaration of crossing the finish line of your first marathon are indescribable. The whole struggle to get there suddenly makes sense. It is a moment of self-affirmation that ranks up there with your greatest accomplishments. And once done, it remains with you. It can never be taken away from you or undone. Ever after, you will have finishing a marathon as a touchstone when facing other challenges in your life. And it is not just the race itself that you can be proud of. It is the whole process of getting ready for the race, setting a lofty goal, and then delivering on your promise to yourself.

As I lay on the grass in front of City Hall, wrapped in my space blanket with my two-year-old crawling all over me and my wife, waiting to see when I might look capable of taking them home, I was thinking, *Hey, I bet I could do better than 3:39. I bet I could at least break 3:30.* Now I'm sure there are a lot of people who finish a marathon and don't plan on ever doing it again as long as they live, but that was not me.

Painful as it was, I had had such a fabulous experience that I resolved to return the next year. In fact, my plan was to make San Francisco my home marathon and return every year. In the months leading up to the race, I would train hard and run like hell in the marathon and hopefully steadily lower my finish time year after year. When I wasn't actively training for the annual big race, I would maintain a strong base and jump into all the local 5Ks and 10Ks around Monterey Bay where I lived to keep up my speed training. That seemed like as much running as I would ever need and as much racing.

But that's not what happened. I went back to San Francisco the next year as planned. We stayed at the Hyatt Regency in Embarcadero Center again where a lot of other runners were staying. I found myself riding the elevator with tall, skinny elite runners. They were discussing how they would choose to drop out of the race if they weren't actually winning. "No use tearing yourself up in the last six miles," one said. I nodded sagely. I contemplated maybe doing a couple of laps around the elevator to demonstrate that I belonged in their club.

The course had changed. I wasn't too happy about that as it threw off my apples-to-apples comparison of my race times from one year to the next, but I decided that it wasn't a big deal…close enough. In fact, the second time around, I didn't lower my time. Maybe absent the excitement of going through the whole training regimen for the first time, I had not put quite as much energy into preparing. I ran hard but ended up taking an extra four minutes over the previous year.

The following year, 1986, I was back yet again, and this time I delivered with a time of 3 hours and 29 minutes. Again the course had changed and my devotion to San Francisco had wavered a bit when I'd gotten wind of plans for a new marathon that would use the Big Sur coast and end in Carmel, California, which was practically in my backyard. But that race was going to require shutting down a huge stretch of Highway 1, which was very controversial and the subject of a lot of debate. Plans for that race seemed sketchy and there was no telling if it would last even if they pulled it off once. Plus I already had a couple of years invested in the marathon in San Francisco. I didn't feel like starting over with another marathon so I passed up participating in the first running of the Big Sur International Marathon.

In 1987, the San Francisco Marathon changed courses yet again, along with some of the major sponsors. Authorities in the city seemed to be constantly reassessing where and when they would allow streets to be closed down for the race. Decisions were changing from year to year and one got the feeling that the race had not stabilized. It turned out that 1984 had been the high water mark for participation in the race. San Francisco wasn't growing into the mega-marathon that had been envisioned.

In 1988, it was time for San Francisco to stumble. I was ticking off my usual 10Ks and starting my series of long runs to get ready for the marathon when I went to register and discovered that the race was not going to be held that year. It wasn't even clear if it was ever going to be held again.

That was it for me. I wanted an annual marathon that I could count on and San Francisco was not filling the bill. It was too late that year for Big Sur, which was in its third year and seemed to be prospering. But I still had reservations about Big Sur anyway. People said the course was very scenic but tough because of all the hills. You were supposed to add ten minutes to your usual marathon time to project your finish time. Since my goal was to set personal records for the marathon, it seemed like I would be shooting myself in the foot by choosing Big Sur as my go-to race. Instead, near the end of the year, I tried the California International Marathon held in Sacramento. It was billed as a fast, net-downhill marathon, a good place to set PRs or to qualify for Boston.

The CIM was a great race and inspiring. Near the beginning of the race, there were some open stretches of country road that took you from Folsom to the outskirts of Sacramento. The road dipped in and out of low spots that were filled with morning fog so you came up to a high point out of the fog and then ran back down into it and then back out.

The other memorable aspect of the race was its end. You finished over a dead straight four-mile stretch through the heart of Sacramento that had one zig zag in it and a hook at the end that deposited you on the Capitol Mall across from the California State Capitol building. The four-mile stretch was a mixture of cityscape and tree-lined residential areas. As I ran along this stretch, I thought I was going to go nuts. It seemed absolutely endless. There were no signs that you were making progress. As far as you could see forward, there were more traffic lights, more trees, more houses, buildings, and, of course, failing, desperate runners. There had been nothing like this in San Francisco where the character of the streets and neighborhoods were constantly shifting and changing and the course was forever twisting and turning.

It was a clear and unmistakable lesson in how critical your mental resources become when you run out of things that might distract you from the pain of a very hard effort. I couldn't sustain myself through the ordeal. Physically I was probably quite capable of soldiering on, but mentally I was wrecked. I told myself I needed a walking break from time to time so I would pick out a traffic light in the distance and walk for a little while after I reached it.

I finally finished about five minutes over my PR time. On that course, on that day, I should have done better. I certainly learned a lot about my mental resources. They were weak and easily scared off. I would need to fix that. I also felt like I still needed to find a marathon that I could do every year. I liked the idea that from year to year I could compare my performance along the way and the finishing time and learn what I needed to improve. San Francisco hadn't worked out and now I was sort of blasé about CIM.

On my way home from Sacramento, driving down California Interstate 5, I found myself mulling over my options. I remember thinking that maybe I'd give Big Sur a try after all.

Chapter 10

On the Edge of the Western World

Reluctantly, I signed up for the 1989 running of the Big Sur International Marathon. It was in its fourth year. I had my reservations. Foremost was the problem of all the hills. Back then, I was totally focused on speed and lowering my personal records for whatever distance I was running. A ten-minute handicap off the starting line for a marathon was nothing to sneeze at. You wanted a course that was going to help you hang on to race pace, not put speed bumps in your way.

Along with a lot of rolling hills, Big Sur was famous for a two-mile climb that came just before the halfway mark in the race. The top of the climb is Hurricane Point at 560 feet. By contrast, the horrifying Heartbreak Hill in the Boston Marathon tops out at 91 feet. You can get to the bottom of the climb up to Hurricane Point under race pace and find at the top that your race pace is shot all to hell. The whole thing is so traumatic that finishers at Big Sur are called "Hurricane Point Survivors."

Then there was the point-to-point, mostly one direction, run-straight-north nature of the course. Living nearby, I'd driven the Big Sur coast many times and the scenery is indeed spectacular, but I was going to be running a marathon. I wasn't going to be sightseeing. Focused on my mile-to-mile pace, anticipating the next mile marker, and dwelling deep in the pain cave, was I going to experience the race as an endless, never-changing asphalt road to nowhere? I couldn't help but think of those long stretches of highway at the California International Marathon and that death march through Sacramento.

Even the weather at Big Sur was a potential problem. Because you run in one direction the whole race and mostly out in the open exposed to whatever winds are blowing off the ocean, a steady headwind coming from the north can plague you for twenty miles. You can also experience a freezing cold start and a warm finish making it hard to get the clothing right. A swing of forty-five degrees Fahrenheit from the start of the race to the finish is not uncommon.

On the other hand, I hadn't heard a single bad thing about the race from runners who had actually run it, so I gave it a try. And it was fabulous. So fabulous, in fact, that over the next 23 years from 1989 until 2011, I ran the Big Sur International Marathon twenty-two times.

Big Sur

The idea for the Big Sur Marathon was sparked by a road sign that Judge William Burleigh, a Big Sur resident, passed as he was leaving Carmel, California, one day headed south on Highway 1. The distance to Big Sur was listed on the sign as 26 miles. Cue the light bulb. The distance on the sign was somewhat arbitrary as Big Sur is not a town per se but rather a region without formal boundaries that stretches 90 miles roughly from Carmel south to San Simeon, site of Hearst Castle.

The original Spanish explorers in the area led by Gaspar de Portolà in their trek north along the California coast had been forced inland to the San Antonio and Salinas Valleys to reach Monterey Bay so they bypassed a large chunk of relatively inaccessible coastline. That area they called *el país grande del sur*, meaning "the big country of the south." The name was later shortened to *el sur grande* or "Big Sur." The name became more or less official when homesteaders in the area asked the government to change the name of their post office from Arbolado to Big Sur in 1915.

The rugged Big Sur coastline where the Santa Lucia mountain range rises abruptly out of the ever-churning ocean is truly a wonder to behold. Fog drifts through the redwood forests above streams and rivers rushing down to the ocean. It's considered a national treasure and called one of the most beautiful coastlines in the world. Cone Peak sits just three miles inland and, at more than 5,000 feet tall, is the tallest coastal mountain in the United States. Inland you find the Los Padres National Forest, the Ventana Wilderness, the Silver Peak Wilderness, and Fort Hunter Leggit. The area was one of the most isolated parts of California until Highway 1 was completed in 1937. Now Big Sur gets about as many visitors each year as Yosemite. The race provides the unique and awesome opportunity to visit 26 miles of this wonderland on foot without the fear of being mowed down by Uncle Rick in a dilapidated camper.

With such a setting, the race held tremendous promise. Burleigh's idea was quite sound. It just needed to overcome formidable logistical nightmares like bussing thousands of runners down to the start, getting aid stations and supplies out to numerous isolated locations, managing a first-class finish area, feeding thousands of runners, getting spent and injured runners off the course safely, turning out thousands of handmade clay awards, and of course getting everyone registered beforehand. Year by year, each of these challenges got solved so runners rarely experienced anything negative at the race.

The first running in 1986 drew 1,800 runners. By 1990, the marathon reached its then-limit of 3,000 runners. (The limit is now up to 4,500.) Along the way, other events were added that allowed runners to choose shorter distances or walk portions of the course. These include a 21-mile run or walk, an 11-mile run or walk, a 12K, a 5K, or running the marathon course as part of a relay team. All these events proved extremely popular. Total participation is now up to 10,000 runners and walkers. There is also a sister race held in the fall, the Big Sur International Half-Marathon, which has also become an internationally recognized event.

A Smashing Success

Quotes from Big Sur runners are collected every year and they run along the lines of "I died and went to heaven." Tommy Owens, for example, writes in 2002, "The best course, support, beauty, details. The best just gets better." *Runner's World* rated Big Sur the best marathon in the country for several years running, but it should be noted that they had a strong affiliation with the race. But look at almost any list of best marathons in the USA from any source and Big Sur will be there. It's been called "one of the best running experiences on the planet," the "best destination marathon in North America," and one of the world's "top ten races to do before you die."

Many of the accolades heaped on the race year in and year out can be accounted for by just the course itself. The race begins in the heart of Big Sur at Big Sur Station in the midst of a classic coastal redwood forest. You roll up and down through the towering redwoods, passing a few rustic eateries and resorts for about five miles before taking a dramatic incline up out of the forest. Then you have open pastures around you with grazing cows and huge green slopes rising on your right and the vast Pacific Ocean on your left. In the distance on a promontory sits the historic Point Sur Lighthouse erected in 1889 to keep ships off the coastal rocks.

After a big sweeping curve at Little Sur River, you climb up to Hurricane Point. From the top you can see about twenty thousand miles in either direction along the coast which is a dreamscape of many-hued blue water, crashing breakers, rocky outcroppings, churning white surf, cypress trees, and parcels of rich green land spilling down toward the water. Bixby Bridge comes next, a Depression-era marvel of engineering set so dramatically across the mouth of a huge canyon that it is one of the most photographed structures in the world.

With the halfway mark of the race in your rearview mirror, you roll up and down along the coast, occasionally getting glimpses straight down to the water's edge or up into the dramatic canyons of the Ventana Wilderness. You pass Palo Colorado Road, Rocky

Bixby Bridge shown from deep within Bixby Creek Canyon where the writer Jack Kerouac once lived and wrote poetry

Point, and Garrapata Bridge before reaching Soberanes Point at mile 19. Soon after, at mile 22, you come to the Carmel Highlands and the first built-up area of the whole course. The wild Carmel estates perched just over the ocean can distract you from the steep hills in this area and sharply cambered roads. Next you pass Point Lobos and run down along Monastery Beach. The more eagle-eyed runners will spot Carmelite Monastery Mission just above them on the hillside that gives the beach its name.

Finally, you push over the last hill, run through Carmel Meadows, and cross the Carmel River Bridge to finish at Marathon Village, a conglomeration of food tents, massage tents, hospitality tents, runner reunion areas, vendor booths, bathrooms, and a beer garden that is all gone the next day.

If you're not into drop-dead gorgeous scenery, maybe the music provided along the way will spark your fire. In 1998, for instance, you had the Robert Louis Stevenson Orchestra performing at the top of Hurricane Point (in a wind that looked like it might sweep them away), the Monterey Brass Quintet at Rocky Point, and the Monterey Youth Orchestra at the Garrapata Bridge. For years, concert pianist Jonathan Lee was set up just beyond Bixby Bridge, playing on a grand piano. The Yamaha concert grand piano is still a staple at the race, but a different pianist has taken over. The amplified sound accompanies you as you cross the bridge and pass the halfway point of the race. You get chills from the emotions you feel.

The music is not all classical. Amazingly energetic and uplifting Taiko drummers are set up at the bottom of the climb toward Hurricane Point every year, giving you a boost to start the climb. You also get rock bands and bluegrass bands scattered along the route, along with a few characters that fire up boom boxes.

Beyond the music, there are whimsical mile markers and volunteers calling out split times and paces. There are eleven aid stations, fully stocked with water and sports drinks, of course, but also with a volunteer holding up Vaseline, another passing out energy gels, and an entire army of volunteers passing out the cups of fluid so you can run right through the aid station. There are crowds of runners cheering you on at the relay exchange points, and a big crowd at the finish to welcome you home.

The massive expo prior to race day is another big plus for the race as are the beautiful pre-race programs and post-race official results booklets. Even the bus ride to the start in the predawn darkness can be a magical experience when the moonlight creates a dreamscape out of the rugged coastline under a blanket of stars. Add in dramatic banks of fog sweeping off the ocean and you can find your pre-race jitters dissolving into a magical mystery tour.

A contented Big Sur resident watching runners go by on race day

So sue me for having this race, of all races, in my backyard and having it readily available to be my go-to annual marathon. For years, race entry was first-come, first-served and the registration form for the next year's race was included in the results booklet. I would peruse the results, check out my time and finish place, read through the articles and runners' quotes, and search for glimpses of myself in the many high-quality photos. Then I'd fill out the registration form, write a check, and put next year's fabulous, guaranteed Big Sur marathon experience in the mail. Of course, nowadays there is a lottery to contend with but there are also tour packages and donation opportunities that can be used to increase your chances of snagging a bib number.

Running the same marathon year after year turned out to be an invaluable experience, a terrific way to monitor both my physical and mental progress as a runner. On the physical side, making comparisons of strengths and weaknesses in my training and execution from year to year was a no brainer. I could watch how my pace progressed from mile to mile and contrast that with past years. I could see what kind of damage the Hurricane Point climb did to my pace and check how long it took to get back to my target pace versus past experiences. I could compare key split times such as at mile 10, at the halfway point, at mile 20, and of course at the finish.

I was also aware of what kinds of feedback I was getting from my body from point to point on the course. At which mile did fatigue start setting into my calves, my quads, or all over? When did I sink down from feeling the pace was manageable to feeling less than human? Where was the wall from year to year? Where did I really falter and want desperately to walk a hill or extend a walking break at an aid station beyond what was actually needed? As the years went by, I became an expert at knowing exactly what to expect at each point in the race.

Going for the PR

The next step was to match up my training for the year with how the marathon played out that year and get a good read on what training had been effective or what training hadn't resulted in any improvements. It was also easy to detect variances in my performance that resulted from unusual course conditions as opposed to being better or worse trained that year. A case in point would be my concerted effort to lower my Big Sur PR time between 1994 and 1997. Race conditions were perfect in 1994; that is, no unusually strong headwinds mid-race or high temperatures over the final miles. I was well trained and could run with abandon. I clocked a time of 3:39:17, my best at Big Sur so far and actually a time that I might have expected. My PR for any marathon was 3:29 from San Francisco, so with the expected 10-minute slowdown due to the difficulty of the Big Sur course, 3:39 looked exactly like what I was capable of when running my fastest.

I had an off training year in 1995 so my time blew up, but in 1996 I was securely back in the hard-training saddle. At the start of the race, I was chomping at the bit and supremely confident that my old course record was in my sights. It's a crowded start at Big Sur with over 4,000 runners blasting downhill on a two-lane highway. I was immediately weaving through runners trying not to get boxed in behind slow starters. I was making a move around one slowpoke when another runner making pretty much the same move but from the other side stepped right into my stride and we tangled badly. I didn't go down but my right foot rolled under and I felt the side of my ankle take a tremendous jolt. I limped to the side of the road as literally hundreds of runners streamed by me. I walked for a while and determined that the leg could be saved, no amputation. Then I began to limp-jog on the shoulder of the road, still being passed by crowds of runners. The pain in the ankle was pretty intense, but I graduated to a run-limp and eventually got to where I was more or less keeping up with the crowd.

It took until about mile five for the pain to fade sufficiently so that I could manage a more or less normal stride and maybe mile ten before I was fully back in the race and able to pull out all the stops. I'd lost a lot of time, of course, but I couldn't help but think about all the hard training that I had put in. Hope springs eternal, so I committed fully to the race and ran as hard as I could.

I crossed the line in a time of 3:39:34, that is, seventeen seconds off my record time.

Coming so close stoked my fire for the following year. I stepped up my training even more. Race day in 1997 came and again I lined up for the start jumping out of my skin. This time, though, I had learned to exercise extreme caution at the beginning of the race. I watched every step until the crowd thinned out. My one concern was that the weather would not cooperate but barring that I knew this year was going to be it. *Sub 3:30,* I fantasized. Knocking a full ten minutes off my previous best seemed within reach.

I blasted through the redwood forest portion of the course and was just at the bottom of the slope where we would climb out of the trees and hit the open pasture lands when I spotted none other than Big Sur Marathon Founder Bill Burleigh standing next to his car, smiling and cheering the runners on. Runners were talking to him as they went by. I was incredibly jazzed up and wanted to say something to him myself. The weather was clear. There was absolutely no wind. I was on my way to a long delayed PR and here was the man who had made all this possible.

"Perfect weather this year," I yelled out as I went by.

Burleigh looked at me and smiled, but then to my great surprise he shook his head. His exact words to me were, "Just wait."

I was puzzled. What in the world was that supposed to mean?

I hunkered down to take the slope up out of the trees. I couldn't wait to hit the section where you look out over the lighthouse. It's usually clear sailing from there over to the bottom of Hurricane Point, and once you're over that and down to the bridge, you're halfway. I was counting just about every chicken I could imagine before even one was hatched.

As I came up the road, I felt it on my head first, then against my chest, and then on my well warmed-up quads. The force of it, now felt up and down my whole body, seemed like a willful, living thing. All forward progress seemed to be cancelled out when my feet left the asphalt, leaving me momentarily airborne, and I was pushed backward. It was a headwind so fierce that it made you feel powerless.

What could I do? Runners were forming lines, drafting off of each other, so I joined in. I could feel myself working extra hard to hold my pace. *It can't last forever,* I reasoned, and tried to give it everything I had. The wind blew on unabated. At the top of Hurricane Point, you could barely advance. The wind was whipping the hats off of runners and right over the side of the cliff without the hat ever touching the ground. Even on downhill stretches, the wind seemed to hold you up as you leaned into the descent. It felt like you were parachuting down the slope.

It was the same on the back half of the course all the way to the sheltered area of Carmel Highlands. It was the strongest, steadiest, longest-lasting headwind the race had ever seen. I charged for the finish totally spent. I knew I couldn't hope to lower my PR significantly on such a day, but I was determined to break it. This time I burst over the finish line with a tremendous gasp. My time was 3:39:44, that is, ten seconds slower than the year before. I had spent over three and a half hours locked in an epic brutal struggle with the wind and come up short yet again by less than a minute. It was a bummer.

On the plus side, though, it made it very easy for me to answer when people asked how fast I was able to run Big Sur. “I can run it in 3:39,” I would answer confidently, “no matter what.”

Chapter 11

The Four Horsemen of the Apocalypse

Going back to Big Sur over and over again certainly allowed me to groove in all my physical responses to running a marathon. Since there was no novelty to the course or the mechanics of being part of the race for me, I could focus wholly on my body's reaction to the pace I set, to the hills, to the wind and heat, and to reaching milestones like five miles, halfway, twenty miles, and the last two or three miles.

In my quest to run faster from year to year, I would micromanage my training and then be able to see the results at Big Sur in my finish time and in how I felt along the way. Of course what I couldn't control was getting older. During my Big Sur streak, I went from age 37 to age 59. (I'm not sure exactly how that happened, by the way.) Advancing through those critical years brought an almost inevitable slowdown in my finish times. I might have fought back, upped my training, and kept trying to run faster, but I didn't. Instead I went through a shift in attitude toward my running. Going faster as my key goal gave way to trying to enjoy the process more; and once again, by doing the same race year after year, I could see exactly how this mental change played out in my experience in the marathon.

The shift in attitude was just one mental adjustment I made in the years running Big Sur. Actually, the things I learned from putting my mental strategies to the test each year was what ended up interesting me the most and helping me advance as a runner, as opposed to the physical aspects of running.

Time in the Pain Cave

With all the long training runs and during the marathons themselves, I certainly spent a lot of time in the pain cave dealing with all the discomforts of pushing myself well beyond my comfort zone. Early on I would say my reaction to pain was quite common. I would try to ignore it. Then I would try to run away from it or deny it was happening. Of course, none of that worked. It just made the pain seem more ominous. I would see the pain as a growing problem. I imagined that it could only intensify until it became unsustainable. This thought would induce fear and panic. Mentally, I would be on a negative downward spiral.

All the fear and panic would cause me to tighten up at a time when staying loose was paramount. I would slow my pace, hoping to relieve the suffering somewhat, or resort to walking breaks. When nothing would make the pain go away, I was left with grimly continuing on to the finish, the minutes seeming to stretch into hours, finding no joy in the run, and feeling badly about the results at the end since I clearly hadn't finished well. Sounds like fun, doesn't it?

This way to the pain cave, or maybe that way, or both ways...

Pain, I learned over the years, requires a much different approach. First and foremost, you must acknowledge it and face up to it. It is part of your reality, part of the present that you are experiencing in the run. Even in this simple act of acknowledging it, you are beginning to rob it of its power. It is not so horrible that you must hide from it. It is not so debilitating that you must ignore it. In fact, the pain is nothing that you wouldn't expect. It springs from the fact that you are pushing yourself to do well in the race. It's a natural thing. You want to say to yourself, *Here it is. Okay, let's deal with it*.

Then it helps to not only face it squarely but to actually sink down into the feeling of it. Embrace it for a while. What exactly is the sensation you are feeling? How intense is it? By picking it apart and taking almost an objective look at it, you are keeping yourself from having an emotional, fearful reaction to the pain. In fact, you can tell yourself to keep the emotions out of it. You are seeking to be objective about the pain, almost as if it were happening to someone else as opposed to you.

Once you allow yourself to fully experience the sensations of the pain—and hopefully recognize that it is not the end of the world, that you are not being asked to storm Omaha beach in Normandy in the first wave on D-Day—then you are able to accept the pain. You may think, well, it's not great but it's also not fatal. I am going to feel this way rather than some other way that I might prefer to feel, but I am okay with feeling this way.

After reaching this point of acceptance, you can try moving your thinking along to other things that are happening to you. What other sensations are you feeling? Where are you in the course and what's the scenery like? How's the temperature? Are you climbing a hill, running down a slope? How are the runners around you doing? What's up ahead? Assess your situation. Do you need to do more drinking? Will you need anything special at the next aid station? Should you be taking an energy gel? As you become engrossed in other sensations, the pain should fade away somewhat and maybe move into the background. If it reasserts itself strongly, so be it. Begin again. Face up to it. Sink down into it. Analyze it and then accept it. Let it fade away once again.

How Bad Can It Be?

An even higher form of acceptance is when you get to a point that you can even laugh at the crummy way you feel. Let's call it gallows humor for the runner, which I think is a very effective way to deal with pain. It can put you into an entirely different mindset. It can bring you from feeling discouraged and defeated to feeling like you're a survivor who can take anything thrown at you. How bad can it be if you can laugh at it?

When it gets bad enough, you might as well laugh.

I often find that when I'm at the most extreme moments during a race, when I'm three miles from the finish of a marathon or ninety miles into a one-hundred-mile run, and it seems impossible to imagine feeling any worse, the whole situation comes across to me as being utterly absurd. After all, I'm in the race and pushing myself all of my own accord. I chose to do this. I put myself in this spot of my own free will. I'm thinking *how stupid could I be,* but I'm also thinking *this is really kind of funny!* I could be home on my couch drinking a cold beer or I could be torturing myself in this marathon, and I chose the latter. Good work! You have to laugh.

Laughing breaks the tension, gets you out of the pity party, and lets you step back for a moment and see yourself from an objective standpoint. What you see is someone who is hurting but also someone who has chosen to be in the fight and strive for something, someone who has gotten off the couch and is reaching for more in life.

A lifelong memory for me was formed once along these lines when I was having problems in a hundred-mile run called Rio Del Lago in California one hot summer. (I wrote about this race at length in *The Tao of Running*.) I probably pushed myself too hard in the afternoon because by evening I was having major stomach issues. I felt nauseous so I didn't want to eat or drink anything, but I had to keep trying to eat so that I would have the energy to keep running. Eventually, I got to the point where as soon as I ate or drank anything, it would come right back up.

This went on all night. I'd get to an aid station, down a cup of Ginger Ale, for example, take two steps, and then throw it all up behind a bush. I'd nibble at an energy gel packet and react immediately with dry heaves. With no food going in and thus nothing to derive energy from, I just kept getting weaker and weaker and slower and slower.

My long-standing running pal and friend David Nakashima was pacing me and he was a saint. He just kept patiently waiting next to me as I threw up. Then he would shuffle down the trail behind me as I weaved and tripped my way along the technical trail we were following. He kept encouraging me to sip at my water supply or try to go back to the energy gel. Finally, we came to an aid station and I thought I might be coming back a bit and the stomach might be settling down. David brought me a cup of broth and I downed it with great hope in my heart and a desperate wish to at last have a few calories inside me to burn. We trotted off. I took about five steps and then my stomach went into violent revolt. It couldn't wait to get rid of the offending broth.

David felt so sorry for me that he reached out and patted me on the back as I bent over the weeds next to the trail and heaved up the broth. When I straightened up, though, instead of once more being stricken with disappointment that I had lost all the calories and might be forced to drop out of the race, I was laughing. David's gesture in patting my back had brought home to me just how incredibly pathetic my situation was. I had been bought so low that David had felt it necessary to reach out and comfort me and that just seemed funny. *Well, it certainly can't get any worse than this,* I was thinking and in the condition I was in, that seemed like a very positive thought.

I was reminded of something that Ann Trason, a legendary ultrarunner and 14-time winner at the Western States 100, once said, "It hurts up to a point and then it doesn't get any worse." In my case, it was more like you can throw up so much and then you can't throw up any more.

As it turned out, I never got over the stomach problems that night. I had to reconcile with moving forward with no energy. It wasn't great but I found I could will myself to do it. I finished in next to last place, but I was under the time cutoff. I have a nice belt buckle to prove it. Much more than the belt buckle, though, I took away from Rio Del Lago that moment when David reached out to pat me on the back and I was able to laugh at myself and transcend the situation.

A Caveat

Here I should mention a caveat regarding pushing on through tough situations and dealing with pain and discomfort. I am talking specifically about the kinds of pains that usually crop up when you are running long and hard. Your quads get sore and painful. You feel totally bereft of energy. Your feet hurt. You are exhausted. You stomach is upset. A blister on your heel is plaguing you. Your skin is chaffing somewhere. These are the types of things that should not stop you or slow you down significantly in a race. They generally do not signal a danger to your health.

If your pain is something that might indicate a more serious underlying problem, an actual danger to your health, then by all means, you should stop until you can rule out any serious issues. Acute and persistent pain, blood in your urine, dizziness, chest pains, and the like are not things to push through but rather signals that you need to get the issue thoroughly checked out and come back to race another day. No finish or target time is worth risking your health over. If you should drop out of a race and it turns out there was actually nothing serious going on, then so be it. No major harm done. Perhaps there was a valuable lesson learned. If you should push through a warning signal and hurt yourself, you might be looking at weeks or months of recovery or even worse a permanent injury that takes you out of running altogether.

But let's get back to talking about dealing with the typical and normal issues that plague you when you try to lower your personal record for a race or take on a new and longer distance such as stepping up to a marathon for the first time or tackling an ultra distance. Every year at Big Sur when I was running hard, I had to cope with those awful last six miles and figure out how to get through them without blowing up.

The Horsemen

Eventually I found my way to four strategies that I think any runner can use to his or her advantage. Let's call them the Four Horsemen of the Apocalypse. They can be summoned at any time during a race or a hard workout, but they really come into their own when the chips are down and the situation has become, at least in terms of finishing your race, apocalyptic. The four horsemen are mindfulness, mantras, music, and moxie.

Mindfulness, of course, we have already explored earlier in this book. It is wonderfully flexible. It can be practiced any time you run, or you can save it for those moments when you desperately need to focus your mind on something other than the pain you are feeling. When being mindful, you focus your attention exclusively on the present, on all the impressions, sensations, thoughts, and feelings you are having at the moment. If you are trying to hold your pace over the last few miles of a marathon, for example, you might focus on the motion of your body, the look of the other runners around you, the camber of the road, the feel of the air, your breathing, the pumping of your arms, the trees along the route, or the many sensations of stress emanating from your lower body.

Thoughts of how far off the finish is or worries about not reaching your goal involve what is going to happen in the future. You should acknowledge those thoughts and then move beyond them and get back to the present. Concern that you have not trained enough or over what happened back at mile ten to slow you down, likewise, are part of the past. They also should be acknowledged and left behind. Focus on just what is happening now. What are the sensations you are directly experiencing right now? The procedures for dealing with pain and discomfort explained at the beginning of this chapter are mindfulness techniques and are readily available to you to help with the painful sensations you might be having.

Using mantras is another technique that we've touched on in earlier chapters. A mantra is particularly useful when you find negative thoughts dominating your mind and you start slipping toward fear and panic. *I can't keep up this pace. The finish is still miles away. The pain is just going to get worse until I can't bear it. I'm going to fail. I should give up and try again on some other day.* Nice logical arguments don't work against such thoughts.

Two of the four horsemen of the apocalypse

Your body is convincing you that your situation is hopeless. You need to block these thoughts with a positive mantra.

The mantra can be just a word, as I explained before, like *patience* or *determination.* Such words remind you of the keys to getting yourself to the end of the race. Or they can be a phrase that is meaningful to you. Early on in my running career, I would tell myself, "Sacred warriors conquer fear and self-doubt." I don't know how I qualified as a "sacred warrior." I don't even remember where that phrase came from, but it made me feel strong and powerful and actually capable of conquering things. It worked for me especially when I was killing it at the end of a 10K. My body would be screaming at me to slow down, but my mind would stay in warrior mode as long as I kept repeating that phrase to myself.

Music is another powerful tool for getting through a race that is closely related in its effect, I believe, to mindfulness. When you introduce music, you are essentially adding another sensation to the present that you are experiencing in your run. In fact, music is a very rich and enthralling sensation with its rhythms and beats, its storytelling, and its strong emotional impact. With music, the present that you are focusing on is a profound experience all by itself as you listen and respond physically and emotionally to the music. It crowds out other sensations that you might be having, such as a strong awareness of your surroundings, which is not necessarily a good thing, but it certainly also crowds out negative thoughts and feelings which might otherwise be undermining you.

Music has the power to distract so much, however, that it becomes a safety issue. Some races ban music so that runners stay aware of their surroundings enough to avoid danger. I always use a single ear bud when I play music so that I'm not cut off from traffic noises on the streets or animal noises in the woods. I also try not to let music become a crutch. I don't want to feel like I can't handle a tough run without music. I want my mindfulness muscle to be strong and then I add the music to enhance it rather than rely solely on the music.

Finally, there is moxie and by that I mean holding an illogical, unreasoning conviction that you are going to keep driving yourself beyond your perceived limits all the way to the finish no matter what. It is really determination by another name, and as I said earlier, I believe it is the one quality that really sets runners who seem to be able to withstand any punishment apart from those runners who eventually fold under the pressure. It's Juma Ikangaa's "will to prepare" and Steve Prefontaine's "guts."

Determination writ large

A Plethora of Problems

In a long race or on a long training run, you often find yourself besieged by not one problem but several issues all at once. Your feet hurt but you are also nursing a slight pull in your calf. It's a lot hotter out than you expected. You can't get cool even when you slow down. Your stomach doesn't feel good because of the heat so it's hard to drink the sports fluid or eat anything solid. It goes on and on. The problems compete with each other to bring you down. You can't fix all the problems. One might relent for a while but others will intensify. Eventually the only thing keeping you going is your moxie, your determination to finish out the race or the workout despite the problems.

Determination is powerful and unreasoning. It's also there when you need it. It's the engine that puts the power behind the notion that you can do more than you think you can do. Getting to it and using it, however, is not a given. It helps to practice by placing yourself in difficult situations over and over so that you get used to summoning your determination. You want the dynamic of success begets success to play out. Once you've used determination to overcome what seemed like an impossible situation, you are better able to summon the determination when necessary the next time around.

Chapter 12

Yo, I Know You're In There

The first running-related pieces I ever wrote were race reports that I sent to *Ultrarunning* magazine back in 2001. The first two reports I sent them they ran without comment. The third report I sent, which was about the 2002 running of the American River 50 Mile, prompted a note from then publisher/editor Don Allison. He said he loved the report, especially the part about the crackheads.

In my report, I had written that American River had really begun for me sometime between two and three o'clock the night before the race. I told the story of being all alone in my motel room fast asleep when I heard a banging on the door of the room next to mine. Then there was a loud voice, "Hey, yo, I know you're in there, yo. Let me in, yo. Open this door. You owe me money, yo. You know you do. Give me my twenty bucks, yo. Look, if you've got Ray in there, that's all right. That's cool, yo. Just give me my money. I know you're smokin' crack in there, yo. You want the cops here, yo? You know this is how it is, yo."

The uproar went on and on. Either there was no one in the room next door or whoever was there was wisely not saying anything. Eventually I phoned the front desk. "We know about the situation," the clerk said. But knowing about it apparently did not mean doing anything about it.

The banging and the shouting continued unabated. "Get out here, yo. I know you're in there. Now I'm tellin' you, yo. You better open this fucking door, yo."

Eventually, the guy left or was taken away but not before I was wired about the whole situation and hardly slept the rest of the night. During the race, the little drama of the night before played out in my mind from time to time. I wrote about this in the race report and how I couldn't help but contrast the lives of those characters chasing each other's twenty bucks with the life I was leading running ultras and feeling the deep satisfaction of finishing a fifty-mile race.

Don Allison probably reacted to my race report because it captured a truth about running that I actually hadn't given much thought to before. Namely, that the running itself is only part of the experience. The full experience of a particular race, or a week of training runs, or any big block of running is the whole constellation of things that happen to you along the way: the run up to the event; the thoughts and feelings you have before, during, and after the running; and the things you take away from the event, the way accomplishing whatever you've accomplished now fits in with the rest of your life.

I noticed this same thing as the years went by running the Big Sur Marathon. The story ceased to be just what happened during the race but widened to include all the experiences I had training for the race: the things my friends and I did the last week before the race as we tapered, the trip to the expo, meeting other runners, pawing through the clothes and equipment at all the booths, talking to the shoe folks, and sampling all the new energy products. After that was the awesome bus ride down to the start in the dark under the stars, trying to stay warm in the staging area before the race, stripping off the warm-ups, and everyone getting their drop bags into the buses that would transport them to the finish.

The race would go by and there would be the great relief at being in the finish area: sitting down, eating something, drinking beer, and exchanging war stories with everyone else. And the experience would last for the next couple of weeks as I adjusted to a new workout schedule that for once was not aimed at the marathon and basked in the glow of having finished the race once again. The point is that the running draws in all these other experiences that impact your life in a myriad of ways. Your running experiences don't just get enriched as you run more; your life experiences get enriched as well.

Try traveling to a race, spending three or four days in a brand new location, going through the whole process of participating in a running event, and NOT having a rich and fulfilling experience. It can't be done. Since I retired, I've had the good fortune to be able to travel all over the country to run and the actual running has become just a small part of the great satisfaction I get from these trips. Landing in cities I've never been to before, driving down fresh highways and getting out on country roads, seeing new areas of the country, meeting new people, and then sharing the drama of the race and the running with a bunch of other like-minded

The full experience of a race involves seeing new places and meeting new people.

runners is just all very rewarding. And you can never predict what you'll encounter or what will be the defining elements of the trip.

A good case in point was my journey to run the vaunted New York City Marathon in 2007. Who hasn't heard amazing things about this race: the crowds, the huge field, the fierce competition, the vibes of the big city, and the celebrities running alongside you? I certainly expected to be wowed by the amazing course that takes in all five boroughs of the city, runs you up and down through Manhattan, and then finishes in the heart of Central Park. That was surely going to be the story I would be telling when I got back home, I thought. But it wasn't.

Instead what really struck me were all the trappings around getting to the start of the race. Isn't that crazy? I wasn't disappointed in the race itself, it's just that the impression I took away from that event that day that will live on foremost in my memory is what happened before we ever took a step running.

Getting to the Start

It's 3:30 in the morning the day of the New York City Marathon. I'm in Manhattan on the Upper East Side, 113th Street to be exact, within spitting distance of Columbia University and not far from the site of Grant's Tomb, the focus of that awful joke, "Who's buried in Grant's tomb?" In the bathroom, the ancient hexagonal tiles under my bare feet are freezing. Ready to go, I venture out into the dark streets with my official orange sweat bag. It makes me feel particularly conspicuous. In the subway I find three other runners with their orange sweat bags arguing over which subway line to take.

Lines 1 or R should go all the way to the southern tip of Manhattan where we need to be to catch the Staten Island Ferry, but the 1 train stops short—torn up stations or something—and the R train veers into Brooklyn just today, according to the Metropolitan Transit Authority website. The lady here in the subway booth confirms that. But last-minute instructions from the race say to absolutely, definitely take the R train. The same instructions warn against the chartered race buses—bridge closings or something—for which about 30,000 people had tickets, so they will have to navigate the subway lines like me.

One of my new friends thinks he has the route figured out so I throw in with him. We get off the 1 train at Times Square where we see a massive crowd of runners heading down the tunnel to the R train. Hmmm...how well do I know my new friend, I ask myself? We go the opposite way and rush through the open doors of the S train. But the doors stay open and we just sit on the unmoving train for about fifteen minutes. Apparently the S train at 4:30 on a Sunday morning follows its own logic. It finally gets off the mark and goes. When we arrive at the 4 (local) and 5 (express) station, we sit peacefully on the platform for twenty more minutes as no trains arrive. Then a 4 (local) train mercifully appears. It's packed with runners and their orange bags. It seems the 5 (express) is not running so we jam onto the 4 (local), which then stops religiously every two seconds. At each stop, we wait as more runners cram on until to compare the thing to a sardine can would be an insult to sardine cans.

Eventually, we arrive at the southern tip of Manhattan Island. A brisk walk takes us from the subway to the ferry building, where we sit on the floor and wait. Waiting has become something of a theme. The ferry crawls in and we watch through glass partitions as people slowly unload. When our time comes to board, we rush down the ramp and cram into the boat like the terminal behind us is on fire. We are, after all, runners who are all jazzed up to run.

The ferry makes its stately way across the harbor, and again we're up, standing in line, waiting to get out. Thousands strong, we rush down a corridor and up a wide stairway where we are stopped in our tracks. We have to wait—big surprise-—for the buses that will shuttle us to the staging areas. A few hundred runners are released onto the buses, then we wait, a few hundred more, wait, a hundred more, wait, wait, wait.

My daughter, Anna, demonstrating her attitude toward a long wait

Once I'm on a bus, the ride is a start-and-stop affair. Other buses block us from the staging area. We wait while they unload. I stare with sleepy eyes at the old wooden houses along the Staten Island streets. At last, we unload near the green staging area. I stumble through green and orange to get to my assigned blue area. It's taken me nearly five hours to get to an empty spot on the grass where I can lie down for a while, freeze in the cold air, and wait some more.

With about an hour to go until the race, I strip down and put my sweat bag into action. How innocently I approach the corridor of numbered UPS vans where the bags must be deposited! A narrowing of the passageway between the trucks has become the focal point of about ten thousand runners trying to pass through. We pack in from both sides and create total gridlock. For a full fifteen minutes, I am lodged in the crowd, which shifts back and forth and side to side. I can see by the edge of the truck I'm near that I'm making no progress. People are shouting, moaning, complaining. Police work the edges trying to help. When I finally reach my assigned UPS truck and throw in my orange bag, I turn and realize I have to go back the SAME WAY.

By the time I return to my cold spot on the ground, it's time to be stood up and put in corrals. More crowds, more jamming together. We wait in the corrals. Now we march in a tight group up the street and out to a big apron of concrete leading to a row of toll booths. Beyond the crowd of 40,000 runners, I see the towers of the Verrazano-Narrows Bridge. I'm so ready to start running I think I'm going to shoot off into space like an Atlas missile, but there is more time to count down. I pray, a little for my family and to stay safe during the race, but mostly that the rest of the time to the start will pass quickly. When the start cannon at last goes off, we walk forward and then trot out on the bridge. The relief of finally running is enormous.

The race itself is okay. You have to hand it to the people of New York. They turn out by the tens of thousands to cheer. Unfortunately, the hard streets quickly find my old injuries: a neuroma in my right foot, a tear in my right calf, a pull in my left hamstring, a weakness in both hips. I cycle through the aches and pains. At the water stations, people trip over each other trying to get to the water. When I stop to stretch out a cramp, people trip over me.

Each borough goes by and we end up back in Manhattan. We run down Fifth Avenue and along Central Park. We make the turn at the south end of the park and head back north toward the finish. I run hard at the end like everyone else. Crowds are cheering.

Then just seconds after crossing the finish line, I have to laugh. I find myself back in a crowd, shuffling along, shoulder to shoulder, toe to heel, waiting. We're creeping up through Central Park waiting to get a bottle of water, waiting for the timing chip to be cut off our shoes, waiting to get to the tables where some snacks are laid out, and then waiting for our orange sweat bags. The running quickly fades in my consciousness. It now seems like it barely happened, or like it was just a brief interlude in the midst of the constant waiting.

The crowds of runners persist up to the greeting area on Central Park West where there are even bigger crowds of runners mixed in with their spectator acquaintances. I return to the apartment where I'm staying on crowded subways and through busy streets. I am alone for the first time in over twelve hours only after I have taken a shower and my friends have left the apartment where I'm staying. The calm and quiet seem fantastically weird, and I can't shake the feeling that I am sitting here waiting for something to happen.

Exactly three weeks later, I'm back home in California, and I've just completed a short, pleasant drive up the coast from Monterey to Woodside, a small historic town not far from San Francisco. Preparation for the start of the Woodside 50K Trail Run unfolds thusly. I get out of my car and walk up a grassy slope to a picnic area. There I stand in line behind one person for less than ten seconds. I get my race number, pin it on my shirt and I'm ready to start. The race director says, "Let's go." That's the start. A little group of us run down a single track trail and we are swallowed up by a giant redwood forest.

For about an hour, there are other runners around but gradually they thin out and disappear and I am running alone. Redwoods rise to majestic heights all around me. The air is crisp and clean. Underfoot the trail is soft, padded with fragrant bay and laurel leaves. One hour melts into another. The trail rising and falling through the forest creates a rhythm. My legs tighten slightly as I ascend, but the downhills are effortless. I feel like I am flying at times. My thoughts soar beyond me and I feel a profound sense of well-being and joy.

I cover the thirty-one miles of trail in a little under six hours. That's about what it took me to get from the apartment in New York to the staging area for the marathon. I can't help but contrast the two experiences in my mind. God bless New York City. The marathon there was a real adventure, but I have to tell you, what I will remember most is that I spent most of the time there waiting to run rather than actually running.

From my trail run, I believe, I'll remember the redwood forest and a profound sense of well-being and joy.

Padding along a trail in the redwood forest near Woodside

Chapter 13

Be Your Dog

There has been a lot so far in this book about mental techniques for dealing with the most challenging parts of running, when you are pushing beyond your comfort zone and striving to reach your potential. We've looked at pain management and how to steel yourself to endure the final stages of a race or a difficult workout.

Of course there is a joy and a profound sense of satisfaction that comes from triumphing over adversity, but there is also a lot of joy to be had from just participating in running and appreciating the whole rich experience of a race or of just an everyday, run-of-the-mill jog in the park. Your frame of mind determines your experience when you're running. If you want to focus on the negative in a run, you will find a lot of things to dislike. If you want to be positive, the same run can supply you with a wealth of great things to be happy about. So let's consider some different frames of mind.

Yet another far-reaching lesson that I learned from returning to Big Sur over and over again was just how different the experience became when I shifted from focusing primarily on running fast to running with the goal of fully enjoying the race and appreciating the experience from beginning to end. Before making this transition, if you had asked me if it was possible to enjoy running a marathon, I would have laughed at the notion. Enjoy a marathon? That would be like asking if you enjoyed having your legs broken.

Back then my conviction was that marathons were invariably hard, very hard. You had to push from the very beginning to get ahead of your target pace. If you didn't, your slowdown later in the race would kill your chances to run a good time. Likewise if you were running uphill, you better push hard to lose as little time as possible. Relax on the downhill? Forget it. On the downhills you had to run hard to make up for time lost on the uphills. Glide over the flat sections of the course? Again, forget it. The flats were where you held onto that faster-than-ever target pace that was going to lower your finish time by five minutes over your previous best. And then the other thing that made the marathon invariably hard was the daunting distance. I couldn't imagine ever being able to run that far without having to dig extra deep.

My attitude toward racing—that is, run as hard as I could and be tremendously disappointed if I didn't have a great race—carried over to most of my training runs as well. Occasionally, I would schedule an easy training day and do a recovery run, but most of the time the training was pushing through hard workouts like tempo runs and intervals on the track. There was no slowing down while I was training if I could help it. I dialed the intensity up to as high as my mechanism would go and kept it there. I did derive a lot of satisfaction from the work I put in and the races when they went well, but there was not a lot of enjoyment in the process.

As the years at Big Sur went by though, as I mentioned before, there was an almost inevitable slowdown as I got older. I would run a good race, pushing as hard as I could from start to finish, but I would still end up five to ten minutes off my best times for the course. With setting new records off the table, I lost the motivation both to train as hard and to race as hard. Of course, ironically the one thing you always heard about Big Sur was that since it was so hilly and such a hard place to run a fast time at anyway, you might as well slow down, savor the remarkable location, and just enjoy the race. It took me about ten years to put that good advice into practice.

The Mind Is Its Own Place

In his great work *Paradise Lost,* John Milton wrote, "The mind is its own place and in itself, can make a Heaven of Hell, a Hell of Heaven." The very first time I slowed down at Big Sur, relaxed, stayed as much as I could in my comfort zone, and ran just by feel, paying little attention to pace or finish time, I realized that for years I had been making a hell out of heaven.

My mind had always been awash in concern about pace, a constant worry from the first step of the race. I had pushed my muscles to soreness and fatigue early in the race so that the balance of the race was run in high pain, always fighting off cramps and totally dead legs. Fear and panic were always just

The author engaged in a mind trick with a plastic flamingo © *Rob Mann*

below the surface as my body gave out. I had no good mental strategies for dealing with the pain back then so the miles and hours were grim. Of course the last six miles were torture. I was spent and just hanging on, trying to contain the damage to my time.

Meanwhile, the sun would be out, the waves would be crashing along the shore, and the light would be sparkling off the water's surface. Music would swell and then fade as we passed by one group of Taiko drummers or piano players after another. Gulls and pelicans would glide by overhead. Sea lions and sea otters would pop their heads out of the kelp just offshore. But if you pay no attention to those things, if you focus only on your pain and panic over the thought that you may not finish under 3 hours and 40 minutes, those things may as well not exist.

Old habits were hard to break, but eventually I learned to focus on my surroundings and put concerns about pace and finish times aside. I ran by feel, keeping the effort just within my comfort zone. I would be off my best times by ten or fifteen minutes, but I could still run the marathon according to my new style in under four hours, which satisfied my lingering need to feel like I was putting in a good effort. Eventually my times started creeping up over four hours, but by that time I was totally over being concerned about finishing times.

I had turned the corner with my running. It had never made sense to me to participate in a race but not be in race mode, meaning run as hard and fast as possible. Why be in a race if you weren't going to run your fastest time and compete? Big Sur turned out to be the ideal place to discover that the experience of the race could be overwhelmingly positive without any regard to the fact that you were part of a competitive event. I had thought that by its very nature a marathon was going to be hell. It turned out that it could just as easily be heaven. My mind was indeed "its own place" and could "make a Heaven of Hell."

Every mile at Big Sur became a new revelation for me. There were a million details in every spot along the route I had passed by over and over again without ever noticing. I became aware of the play of light and shadow in the fields, up in the mountains, and on the water along the shore. I caught all the minor variations in the wind, the temperature, and the moisture in the air along the way. I was alive to all the runners around me. I could feel their reaction to this wonderful place, their joy and astonishment at arriving at the top of Hurricane Point. I caught the vibe of Big Sur being a huge shared experience with all the other runners.

The distance ceased to be so daunting. I ran relaxed so my strength and energy lasted well into the final miles. I had a lot more perspective in my reaction to my muscles growing tired. There was no emotional response to aches and pains cropping up. Instead of experiencing panic and fear at the notion that I would fall short of a goal, I would simply tell myself to slow down and take it easy. There was no rush anymore. Going the whole twenty-six miles stopped being such a big deal for me. It was easy.

If you haven't made this shift in your running, going from focusing on the results to focusing on the process of the run along the way, you should try it. Sign up for a race but leave behind your usual target goals and stretch goals. Just run to enjoy yourself and stay in your comfort zone as much as you can. You'll be amazed at how much easier the race seems and how much more you enjoy being there. Make your own hell into a heaven.

A Dog's Perspective

Changing gears here, let's explore another possible frame of mind that you might want to try. I am the lucky owner of two dogs, although if you asked them, they would tell you that they own me. They are both Chihuahua mixes. We didn't go to the local SPCA shelter looking for Chihuahua mixes but when we got there, it was solid Chihuahua mixes as far as the eye could see. Apparently some notable Chihuahua appearances on TV and in movies had made them very popular so at least here in California we are experiencing a Chihuahua glut.

Anyway, we are now providing a home to Hermes and Sebastian, who seem very happy with the arrangement. Hermes, the older of the two dogs, appears to be a Ratcha, a mix between a Rat Terrier and a Chihuahua. He is very small but he has a beautiful coat of brown, white, and black. He gives the impression of always being polite and extremely well dressed. Sebastian is a mix of who knows what. He has stubby crooked legs, a wonderfully expressive face with a top lip that hangs up just a bit so that his front teeth are slightly exposed when he looks at you. It makes you believe he is a deep but pensive thinker. His coat is shiny black with a nice white blaze on his chest. He's got a thick, tightly curled Pug tail. When he takes a stand, he looks like a tiny bull.

Hermes is shy. Sebastian is like a small bull in a small china shop. Both love going for a walk above anything else. It is their attitude toward the walk and their conduct on the walk that bring them into the pages of this book. From the time they have breakfast until about ten in the morning they sleep on the couch like the dead. Nothing can rouse them. But as the time for their first walk of the day approaches, they emerge from their blankets, yawn and stretch, and begin putting me under microscopic examination.

As I pass through the room, they jump up on the back of our sectional couch and watch me carefully, ears erect and tails waving slightly. If I get coffee and go back to the library, they relax and lay back down in whatever patch of sunlight they can find. But as soon as I reappear, they're on guard again. They watch my face. Am I looking directly at them? Am I speaking with that "we're going on a walk" tone in my voice?

If I go toward the bathroom or the garage, they start running around and nipping at each other. A walk usually comes after a

Hermes and Sebastian lobbying for a walk © *Anna Dudney*

bathroom visit or a trip to the garage to put on outdoor shoes. I announce my intention to walk and they explode. Sebastian gets up on his hind legs and leaps up and down. Hermes jumps onto the settee next to the front door and tries to bite my hands as I reach for their leashes inside the front closet door. Hermes chews on Sebastian's leash as I attach it to Sebastian's collar. We shoot out the door and I have to run a full block with them before they calm down enough to walk.

Their attention to the sights, sounds, and smells along the sidewalk where we're walking is laser-focused and complete. They race up to a key landmark along the way, a tree trunk, where they carefully smell all the messages left there by other dogs before leaving their own calling cards. A quick sniff dismisses a juniper next to the sidewalk but a patch of grass on the next lawn garners very meticulous attention. The movement of some blackbirds landing in a tree half a block away catches Sebastian's eye. He pulls me in that direction. Hermes has long ago assigned birds to a No Relevance to Me category so he continues canvasing the grass.

We exit the residential area and emerge onto a Bureau of Land Management park where I release the dogs from their leads. They race off up a trail but then a scent stops them cold. They both work over a clump of weeds before trotting further up the trail. As usual, I am mesmerized by how they move, how their legs and paws work, propelling them with perfect efficiency along the trail. I try to imagine just how they are experiencing this walk. Their minds must be given over completely to the sensations reaching them through their senses, especially to the rich and vibrant smells flooding in on them. I would imagine that they're totally unaware of their bodies' movements. They speed up, slow down, stop, twist, or roll on their backs to cover themselves in a scent. It's probably all unconscious, just automatic reactions that have the purpose of getting their noses in the right position or helping them smell or spot another dog in the distance.

In fact, it's like they're practicing an advanced form of mindfulness. Their focus on the rush of sensations flowing into their minds is total. This stream of sensory information is uninterrupted by concerns about something that happened the day before or worries about what might happen next in their lives. Perhaps with dogs such ideas are never there to begin with, but definitely, out in the field they don't seem concerned about anything that isn't dead in front of them. With no regard to the physical act of running or how they are moving and with no ideas about the past or future to distract them, they must experience the present as wholly the sensations that they are receiving. It must be a deeply satisfying way to feel for them else why would they so obviously prize this experience of going for a walk so much?

They get fed at the end of their evening walk every day so the pattern of going on the evening walk and then immediately being fed must be quite clear to them. And of course, eating dog food pushes all their excitement buttons just like walking. Yet near the end of the evening walk, if I veer off the usual route and take them down a path leading away from home, they are thrilled.

Any impulse they may have to get back home to eat is fully trumped by this chance to get more walk.

So here is my suggestion. Be your dog. Do some extreme mindfulness training where you attempt to run and focus

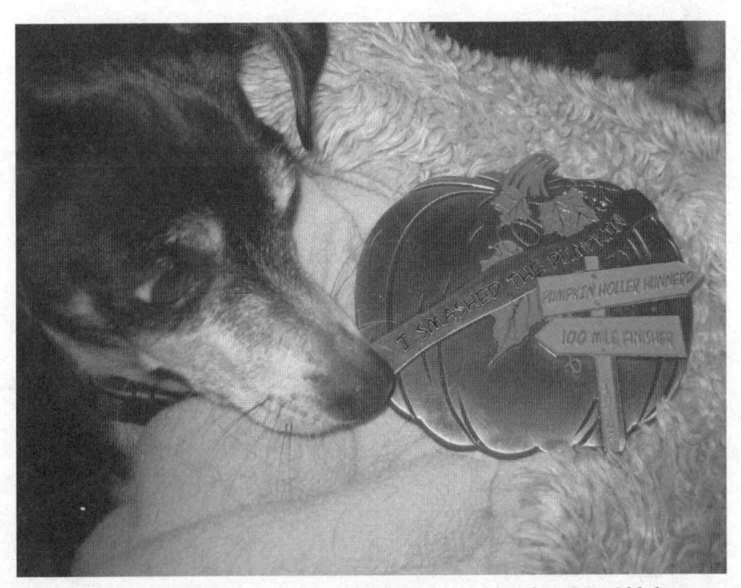

Hermes inspecting a suspicious belt buckle obtained in faraway Oklahoma

completely and exclusively on the input from your senses. Pay attention to what you are seeing and drink in the new sights with each turn of the trail. Focus on the smells. Try to sort out individual smells from the mixture of smells. Listen for every bird song, every random noise, the sound of your footsteps and your breathing. Feel the air on your skin, and of course, feel the motion of your body. Channel distracting thoughts quickly to the back of your mind and return to experiencing the present. See if you begin to develop a sense of flow. See if time and distance begin to go by less noticed or not noticed at all.

You can even imagine that you *are* your dog as you run along. Imagine that the sensations pouring in on you are all that you are aware of. You're not thinking of anything else at all. You're not even thinking about being on a run or running at all. You are just existing in the present and your being is the sum total of the sensations that you are feeling. It's a pretty radical notion but I think very interesting to explore. Try it and see how it goes and how you feel afterwards.

Unusual Mental Territory

Run far enough and long enough, run overnight, or run a multi-day stage race and you may find yourself entering into some very unusual mental territory. Couple exhaustion with the very early half-light of dawn and you can get your mind conspiring with your eyes to play all sorts of visual tricks on you. Or a tired mind can work solo to make you believe things about your situation that are not true or go one step beyond and simply cause you to experience bizarre hallucinations.

Hundred-mile races often create just the right conditions for visiting these more colorful places in your mind. You've got exhaustion, check; running overnight, check; jerky, shadowy lighting conditions all night, check; murky half-light at dusk and dawn, check; severe sleepiness, check; and an irrational mind in control of the whole situation. After all, you did choose to run one hundred miles, how rational was that?

I've run a lot of hundred-mile races and right from the start I was very susceptible to my eyes playing tricks on me. After running all night, as soon as the first light would start filtering through the trees in the forest, I could focus my gaze on just about anything and it would start reforming itself into something odd or ominous. If I stared at the tangled branches of a tree, for example, I'd soon find a cougar crouching there looking back at me.

Nothing was too bizarre. A bunch of tree stumps scattered out over a forest floor became an army of robots buried up to their chests in the ground. Visions would morph from one thing into another. A classic example of that happened to me early one morning in the Washington National Forest during the Massanutten Mountain Trails 100-Mile Run. I was trotting down a single track in a thick part of the forest. I'd just judged that there was enough light that I didn't need my flashlight anymore. I looked up and way off in the woods I could see a long horizontal mass with something sticking up behind it.

Much to my surprise, my eyes focused in on a pair of girls with long hair sitting there in the forest behind something like a baby grand piano. My exhausted mind tried to make sense of what I could clearly see, and I lit on the notion that the crazy race staff had put them out here to surprise us with a little

Is it just me, or do you see a bear's head emerging from this tree?

music as we got near an aid station, which I suspected must be just around the bend.

No sooner had I figured that out when, as I got closer, I could see that it wasn't two girls behind a piano at all, it was a scruffy guy in a leather jacket with very long hair flowing out behind him sitting on a great big chopper style motorcycle. I couldn't imagine where he'd come from, maybe from a nearby dirt road that I couldn't see, but it looked like he was there waiting to say hi to a runner he knew in the race. Only, in fact, as I came still closer, I realized I'd been mistaken again. There was no motorcycle guy at all. What I was seeing, very clearly and unmistakably, was a dolphin leaping up over a wide breaking wave that was washing through the forest. This at last stumped me. Even my wildly protean mind couldn't come up with a plausible explanation for a wave being here in the middle of the forest.

Finally, a few steps more brought me right up to the dolphin and the wave. The wave was a long chunk of tree trunk lying on the ground forming a horizontal mass. The dolphin was a small bushy tree sticking up behind the tree trunk.

Encountering these visual tricks at 100-mile races became so frequent and so commonplace for me that eventually I learned to just ignore them. I will even confess to getting to the point where I even welcomed them and enjoyed them. As long as they weren't too scary, they were wonderfully diverting.

Then there were instances that didn't involve visions but were something else. A case in point would be something I experienced near the end of the Mohican Trail 100 in the summer of 2016. This time the light was not an issue. It was around high noon on day two of the run and I remember being on a trail coming through an open area where the vegetation had grown up to about chest high. I couldn't have been more exhausted and sleepy. I was running along, fighting to keep my eyes open.

As I followed the trail, I felt this weird hypnotic effect resulting from me being down in the trough of the weeds and rocking back and forth as the trail jogged right and left. Gradually, I lost all notion of being in a race. I knew I was running, yes, but I was running to get to a German bookstore where I was supposed to meet my daughter. I had a vague sense that someone was following me, I had just passed another runner, but all I knew was that this person shouldn't be allowed to catch me. The important goal, though, was getting to the German bookstore. I was all full of warm feelings for my daughter and couldn't wait to see her.

I can't tell you how long I spent running to the German bookstore.

It felt like a very long time, but I can say with certainty that as long as I was on my way to the bookstore I had absolutely no sense that I was in a 100-mile footrace. At last, a structure appeared up ahead. I fully expected it to be a charming little shop of exposed beam, wattle-and-daub construction, sitting next to the trail. There'd be a display window of leaded glass with books with Gothic print on their covers propped up inside.

But instead the structure was a pop-up canopy with a camp table underneath covered with big water jugs, paper cups, and things to eat. Several people were standing around, including some runners dressed like me with numbers attached to their shirts or shorts. I recognized at once that it was an aid station and, seeing it, I connected back up to the fact that I was in a race.

Gatekeeper for the land of strange and unusual states of mind

I can't explain the illusion of the German bookstore and the meeting with my daughter. I think it is possible that I was actually in some kind of quasi-sleep state even as I continued running and that I was dreaming at the same time. My experience normally when I fall asleep on my feet is that I stumble and immediately wake back up. But completely losing the notion that I was in a race and having such a strong alternative world going on in my mind was strange beyond belief.

Strange visions and hallucinations are not exactly frames of mind that you would choose for yourself, but be aware that they may lie in wait for you if you push yourself hard enough. The other frames of mind we looked at are there for you any time you choose. Run with a focus on enjoying the process rather than always trying to give your maximum performance. You may realize that enjoying the process is actually the point after all. And play around with the notion of being your dog. You may find that running is a different animal than you thought all along.

Chapter 14

Prairie Runner

Let's pick up on the concept from the previous chapter concerning the strange places your mind can go when you run, especially when you run yourself into a state of exhaustion. Most of the things in the story that follows happened to me just as I describe them, but I did massage events a little and I added some "texture." What is definitely true, though, is that in the act of running a very long and hard race in the Flint Hills of Kansas I learned some very important things about myself. Of course, I would ask: Who hasn't done a lot of running and not at some point learned a lot about themselves?

The Story

It was hard to say which was worse: the ache in my legs, the pulled muscle throbbing in my back, the headache, the nausea, or fighting constantly to stay awake as I weaved from side to side on the gravel road. I'd run plenty of long races before, but this first try at a hundred miles was killing me. I'd spent all day crossing the Flint Hills of eastern Kansas baking in the sun and fighting a stiff headwind, which the locals jokingly called "Kansas mountains." Now the night and sheer exhaustion were doing me in.

The floodlamp cast a garish light over the aid station at Matfield Green. The camp chairs lined up next to the aid table threw an ominous row of shadows across the road. A pair of crumpled runners covered with blankets filled two of the chairs. Neither was moving. They looked done, along with another guy stretched out on a cot behind them. It bucked me up a little that at least I was still on my feet.

The aid table was littered with cups, sticky chunks of watermelon and cantaloupe, and some cut-up peanut butter and jelly

One road leading out to the prairie in eastern Kansas

sandwiches. None of it looked edible with my iffy stomach. The cut-up sports bars, just the thing for failing runners, looked particularly bad. I couldn't touch them.

I collapsed into a chair beyond the table as far away from the spent runners as I could get.

"Well, blow me down," my sister said, standing over me with a sandwich in one hand and a cup of soup in the other. "Aren't you a sight? You need a blanket? It's gettin' cold out here."

She had on a thick jacket and a wool cap. I was still in just a shirt and running shorts, the same clothes I'd had on since early morning. The exertion was keeping me warm even in the cool night air.

"I'll put on my warmer shirt," I said, "but no blanket. If I get too comfortable, I'm finished."

She handed me the soup. I tried a sip. It was potato soup, thick and salty. I set the cup down in the dust at my feet and rested my head in my hands. The harsh light made everything look slightly unreal, like I was watching a movie. The noisy throbbing of the generator powering the light merged with my headache. Somewhere up the road, some idiot was laughing.

"How much farther?" I asked.

"About twenty miles," she said. "You're almost there."

I half laughed, half snorted. Twenty miles was still a very long way. I drank a little more soup and waved the sandwich away. My stomach was dead set against anything solid. My sister had fished a shirt out of my bag, so I struggled into it. After a while, I stood back up. I felt dizzy. I closed my eyes and hoped the dizziness would pass.

"Here're your bottles," she said. "Sports drink in one, water in the other." She shoved them into the pockets in my running belt. "Take care of yourself out there."

I started off.

"Wait!" someone yelled, "Did you get fresh batteries?" A tug at my arm stopped me cold. I handed my flashlight over. This was a disaster averted but it hardly registered on me. I could have been stuck out in the dark with no light, miles from anywhere.

"Thanks," I said. The new batteries made a big difference. Instead of a dim spot of light barely showing me where my feet were about to hit, the road was all lit up. Crisp, jagged shadows bounced around my legs as I moved forward. The fringe of bluestem grass that covered this part of the Kansas prairie hung over the side of the road and glowed silver in the light.

"I can do this," I mumbled to myself.

I hadn't gone far when I heard footsteps behind me. Or did I? Was it just the full water bottles bouncing up and down in the pockets on my belt?

Someone pulled up beside me. I half turned and got the shock of my life. "Dad?! My God, what are you doing out here?"

He ducked his head and smiled, happy that his little surprise had worked out. He reached over and patted me on the back. Just like my dad to spring this on me. He knew how tough this was going to be for me and decided to help. But it was a miracle for him to have recovered enough from his stroke to be out here running in the middle of the night. I had no idea he'd made such progress. It looked like the paralysis on his right side was gone except for maybe a little hitch in his step.

"Is this safe for you?" I asked him. "It's great you're here, but I can make it alone if I have to."

He shrugged and plugged along, stubborn as always. I wasn't going to talk him out of something he'd decided to do. I looked over at him. His gray hair stuck out from under his cap. Deep wrinkles creased his face. And yet the old spark was there. I saw it in the tilt of his head, the determined way he was keeping up with me.

It reminded me of the summers when I used to shag golf balls for him. He'd hit a hundred balls without a break except to switch clubs. And then if he wasn't happy with his swing, he'd hit a hundred more. I'd stand there with my baseball glove catching the balls in the web until he got to his long irons. Then they'd be coming in too hot to handle. I'd take them on the bounce. By the time he got to his two iron, he'd be just a little figure way off over the long stretch of grass. I'd see his motion through the ball and then, after a long pause, I'd hear a nice solid "thwock." The ball would rise up and come straight toward me like it was shot from a gun. I'd hardly have to move a foot left or right to snag it.

Since he wasn't saying anything, I assumed he still wasn't talking. I asked him.

He looked over at me, shook his head. No luck there. After the stroke, he'd worked with a speech therapist for months but never got beyond just a few words.

"Guess I'll have to do the talking," I said. "Actually, I'm glad you're here. I sort of have some stuff I'd like to get off my chest." He glanced at me. "I mean when you had your stroke, it was such a shock. One day you were there and I was just a kid in high school, and then, bang, you're in the hospital. I didn't know what to do. I never had to deal with anything like that before. And I just…I don't know…looking back I just couldn't face up to it. I guess I didn't want to give up the life I had. It probably looked to you like I didn't care much or something."

He reached over and put his hand on my shoulder, gave it a squeeze to show me he understood.

"And I know I wasn't any picnic back then. You couldn't tell me anything. I always thought I was right. But now I know I was just stubborn. I guess that apple didn't fall far from the tree, did it?"

Dad smiled at that. He'd never hidden the fact that he took a lot of persuading himself.

"I wish it had been different, Dad, that we could have talked more once I grew up, about your service and what not. I remember when we were little kids you used to say, 'Hit the deck' to get us out of bed, or you'd say, 'All ashore that's goin' ashore,' or 'Smoke 'em if you got 'em,' all that Navy stuff. God. 'Smoke 'em if you got 'em.' I didn't even know what that meant."

I stopped talking. I thought I might be embarrassing him. The noise of the gravel crunching under our feet filled up the silence.

"The fact is I wish I'd been a better son. You were so brave facing up to that stroke. I realize that now. You couldn't talk to me about what was going on in my life but actually you were showing me the way the whole time."

He looked at me and nodded to show me he'd understood. Then he threw a playful punch at my shoulder, sort of a signal that I should lighten up some. "Okay," I said. "That's it. I'm done. Enough said."

I went back to focusing on moving forward. There were all sorts of odd little noises coming out of the prairie around us: whirrs, buzzes, muffled screeches, low screams, howls, hisses, clicks, groans. The dark grasslands all around us looked perfectly still, but it sounded like there were animals everywhere. "Hear all that?" I said. He nodded. He hunched up his shoulders and made a face as if he were scared.

That made me laugh. Just then a bright line streaked across the sky in front of us causing us both to look up, a shooting star. "Unbelievable, isn't it?" I said, looking at the stars. Out here there was nothing to block the sky: no trees, no ridges, no mountains, no buildings, nothing. The stars stretched overhead and came right down to the flat horizons all around us. The Milky Way was as clear and distinct as a highway. Miles away there were a few scattered lights just above the horizon: the blinking red lights of a radio tower, a bright light bobbing up and down on an oil derrick, a pair of white lights marking a grain silo, and, twenty miles away, a faint dome of light over the town of Emporia.

We settled into a rhythm. Whenever the road sloped up, we fell into a brisk walk. When the road sloped down, we went back to a slow jog. On the flat parts, we did whatever I could manage, some running, a lot of walking. From time to time, rabbits would appear on the side of the road. They seemed strangely unafraid, like they were used to people running by in the middle of the night. A coyote started to howl. Then a whole chorus of them joined in. It made goosebumps stand up on my arms.

"I'm glad you're here," I said. "I'd hate to be alone with that going on."

Aid Station

After what seemed like an eternity, we saw some lights up ahead. Slowly, the canopy of an aid station formed up in my confused vision. At first, it looked like several people standing around

Aid stations seem to materialize out of nowhere later in the race.

in front of it, but as we got closer and the light got stronger, the group resolved into just two people.

We pulled up and the guy standing there said, "Have a seat, old timer."

I shot a glance at Dad. I knew being called that would rankle him. He gestured for me to take the chair instead.

"Where's your friend?" I asked.

"I'm alone out here, buddy," he said. "Nobody else was crazy enough to be out here in the middle of the night."

I realized my eyes were playing tricks on me. There hadn't been anyone else, but I had a vivid impression of a girl with the hood of the sweatshirt she was wearing pulled up over her long hair.

"You okay?" the aid station guy asked.

"Gettin' through," I said. "Thanks to my dad."

"Okay," he said. "Try to eat something. There's soup. The cookies are good. Don't hurry. You've got lots of time." The guy checked his watch. "You've got hours and it's only just a little over ten miles to the finish. You'll make it. Just stay upright and mobile."

I nodded. Dad pushed a cookie in my direction. "Feed your stock before you feed yourself?" I asked him, smiling.

"What's that?" the aid station guy said.

"Nothing, just something my dad always used to say."

I tried to bite into the cookie. I still couldn't eat. It felt like it would just come back up. I waited awhile and then got up. If I couldn't eat, there wasn't much point in staying. "Better move along. Don't want to get stuck in this chair."

The aid station guy helped me with my water bottles. "Take care," he said. "You sure you don't want some soup?"

After we'd gotten out of earshot of the aid station, I said, "Nice guy, but I didn't like his cookie." We chuckled together. Making the joke seemed to lift a burden off my shoulders. I felt the exhaustion and soreness recede just a bit.

A little farther down the road, some dark shapes loomed out of the night in front of us. I flashed my light over and caught the broad placid face of a cow staring back at me. There was no fence here so the cattle were scattered right across the road. We slowed to a walk and tiptoed through the middle of them.

After that, things went downhill fast. Both my ankles started hurting. I loaded up on painkillers, but they were having no effect. I couldn't run anymore. Each step I took was torture, even at a walk. We had left behind the rolling terrain of the Flint Hills now and were on straight flat roads that led back to the little town where the race had begun. An endless barbed wire fence lined both sides of the road. I wasn't seeing any of the markers for the course anymore, no chalk, no ribbons. Dad was looking out for them, too, but they just weren't there. Plus we hadn't seen any other runners for a very long time, maybe hours. I began to think that we'd taken a wrong turn and had gotten onto some random road going nowhere. Every light I saw in the distance I would imagine were the lights of a town, but we'd get closer and I'd see that it was just a single light hung on a barn over an empty farmyard.

"I don't think I'm going to make it, Dad," I groaned. "I'm falling asleep on my feet. I think I need to sit down for a while."

The next thing I knew, I was sitting on the road. Maybe I'd fallen down. Dad was tugging on my arm, trying to help me up, but I felt totally beat. "Just go on," I said. But Dad kept pulling. I looked up at him. He looked desperate to say something, but of course he couldn't.

But then he did anyway. His voice creaked like an old hinge. "No!" he said. "No, no, no!"

The sound of his voice shocked me. It reached me like nothing else could have. I struggled to turn over onto my hands and feet. My head was spinning, but I managed to push myself back up to my feet. "Okay," I said. "I'll try."

The night seemed at its darkest and coldest. Moving forward was like pushing through a thick wall. I was desperate to find some sign that we were at least still on the right road. My light had dimmed, so again there was just a weak pool of light dancing over the gravel in front of me. The road went on and on. The pain in my ankles was relentless.

I'd lost all hope and was ready to beg Dad to let me stop when we came to a turn. There was a white arrow on the road clearly marking the turn onto a blacktop road. I couldn't believe it.

"This is it," I said. "The only blacktop we ran on was right at the beginning of the race. We're almost there." I looked up and could see a few lights ahead and more lights scattered along the road further up. It was the edge of town.

For the first time in hours, I broke into a jog. I forgot all about the pain in my ankles. "We made it, Dad." I was saying. "I would have quit way back there but we made it." Way off on the horizon I could see the first faint glow of dawn dimming the stars in the east.

"C'mon, Dad," I yelled. "C'mon." I felt like I was flying now though I was probably barely moving. I saw people up ahead gathered in the road. I went by someone who called out my race number.

"Lookin' good," the person yelled after me. Then people were reaching out to stop me. Several green glowsticks tied to a post marked the finish. I was done.

Finish Line

My sister ran up and gave me a big hug. When she let go, I almost fell. She had to prop me up with her hip. "Good job," she said.

"Can you believe it?" I said. "What a night!"

She shook her head. "Running all night at your age, I declare!"

"Well, having Dad sure helped…" I started to say but then I stopped. I focused on my sister. It was like I was seeing her for the first time after a long, long separation. She had the same hairstyle she'd always worn but her hair had gone gray. Her mouth had widened and turned down. Her skin was wrinkled and splotched. "What the…"

An abandoned barn on the edge of town

I gasped and turned to look back down the road. There he was. I'd left him behind when I rushed to the finish line but he was still coming. Only he was different. He was dressed differently. His running clothes were gone. He wore the striped pajamas my mother had bought for him when he first came home from the hospital. There was a cane in his left hand. His useless right arm hung down his side and jerked as he moved. The fingers on his dead hand were splayed out over his right thigh. He stepped forward carefully with his left leg and then swung his right leg forward. A brace attached to his right shoe kept his foot straight and his toe up. He was looking at me and smiling, although now the right side of his face drooped so that only one corner of his mouth rose.

"Sorry, it's just me here," my sister was saying. "Your whole family's back at the motel, asleep. The kids sure wanted to watch Grandpa finish, but they only lasted until a little after midnight."

A young woman standing next to us had overheard, "Grandpa? Awesome! I bet you're the only grandpa out here. What in the world made you want to run a hundred miles?"

I looked back up the road again. The light was growing fast. There were wide fields on either side of the road filled with the stubble from a harvested corn crop. I could see all the way back to where we had made the last turn onto the blacktop road. And the road was empty. No one was there.

I bent over, put my hands on my knees to support myself, and burst into tears.

My sister patted me on the back. "Let's get back to the car. You need to get to the motel and get into bed." I kept crying as she led me away.

"Well, you big baby," she said. "You finished the race. It ain't nothin' to cry about."

Chapter 15

Once Upon a Time

California's Western States 100-Mile Endurance Run is the iconic race for long-distance trail runners. The granddaddy of 100-mile trail runs in the United States, it begins in Squaw Valley near Lake Tahoe, passes through the high country of the Sierra Nevada, and ends in Auburn just up the highway from California's state capitol, Sacramento.

It is so popular that long ago a lottery system was required to equitably award the 370 or so starting slots to the thousands that apply to run the race. In 2017, the probability of a runner being chosen who had only a single ticket in the lottery (the more often you apply and are not chosen, the more tickets you get) was just 2.5%. Years ago, a runner's chances in the lottery were about fifty-fifty. Plus you were automatically awarded a starting spot if you failed to get chosen two years in a row and then applied for a third year. Nowadays it can take years to get a chance to run there. Once you get there, you want to make it as great an experience as it can be.

About halfway through Western States, the lucky runners who did manage to wrangle a bib number pass a crusty old wrought iron gateway standing by itself deep in the forest. The lettering on the gateway spells out "Deadwood Cemetery." There is a short side trail that climbs up to the graveyard situated on a lofty bluff overlooking El Dorado Canyon. You might think that at least a few runners would be so intrigued by this sign of the area's colorful Gold Rush past that they would go have a quick look, but nobody does as far as I know.

Now imagine a runner passing by the Deadwood Cemetery gateway who already knew all about it, knew how the ghost town of Deadwood came to be, where it fit into Gold Rush history, what the term "deadwood" meant to early prospectors, knew that Sam Colt once lived in Deadwood, and knew something about the members of the Ebbert family who are buried there. The runner might even know who Drucilla Barner is and how her foundation plays a substantial role in keeping the trail under the runner's feet preserved and maintained.

Wouldn't that runner's rich experience as he or she passed by that gateway be in sharp contrast with the runner's experience who knew nothing of the area, had no associations to make, and who perceived the spot as only another chunk of trail that had to be grimly endured? Now imagine that Deadwood was just one spot among many that our knowledgeable runner would be visiting during the race that rang with associations and provided a fascinating context for all his or her experiences that day.

Here is another possibility for a mental framework that one can adopt in a race or even during one's weekend run near home. Run with at least a portion of your mind engaged with thoughts

A view of El Dorado Canyon

of the area's past or present. Some races present this opportunity in a big way. Imagine any of the major city marathons—New York, Boston, Chicago, Los Angeles—in this context. Spend an afternoon with a course map and you could read up on a hundred locations along the route that you will be passing that are rich in stories and history. Then on race day you'll have all those possibilities for diverting your thinking away from the rigors of the race and onto the landmarks you're seeing.

Less well known locations may seem less promising for this treatment but you would be surprised at what treasures a little research on the Internet can uncover about a place. For example, I signed up for a trail run in North Carolina in the Uwharrie National Forest. I'd never heard of it and couldn't find anyone else who had, even among past residents of North Carolina. I didn't know how to pronounce "Uwharrie" and had no clue as to what the word meant. Frankly it didn't look like such a promising place to get to know, but after a little research, I realized I was dead wrong.

Uwharrie (pronounced *ooh-whari*) turned out be the name of one of the many Native American groups that had made their home in the thick pine and hardwood forests of the area dating back 10,000 years. In fact, the rolling forest floor was actually the remnant of an ancient mountain range, one of North America's oldest that had its origin an astonishing 400 million years ago. The nearby town of Albermarle is full of much more recent history, including being the birthplace of *American Idol* finalist Kellie Pickler. But the most surprising thing I learned about the area was that among Sasquatch or Bigfoot enthusiasts, the Uwharrie National Forest is practically ground zero. There have been more reports of Sasquatch sightings there than in any other area of the country. Who knew? Suffice it to say that my thoroughly marvelous run in the Uwharrie National Forest was full of thoughts of Sasquatch and Kellie Pickler.

Storybook Trail

Let's return to a consideration of the Western States 100-Mile Endurance Run. It is certainly a prime example of how investigating the history of an area beforehand can provide rich material for thought during the race. Moving from start to finish, the history of the Western States Trail unfolds like a storybook.

Western States begins at the base of the Squaw Valley USA ski resort, home of the 1960 Olympic Winter Games. These were the first games to be nationally televised and the first to use computers to tabulate results. Walt Disney organized the opening and closing ceremonies. Squaw Valley shot from obscurity to one of the most recognized ski playgrounds in the world. Yet a mere five years before the games were held there, the area boasted only a single chairlift and two rope tows. Promoter Alexander Cushing traveled the world selling International Olympic Committee delegates on the mystique of the California valley with its annual snowfall of 405 inches. The poor Austrians were so sure Innsbruck would get the nod for 1960, they started assigning living quarters to athletes. St. Moritz and Garmisch-Partenkirschen lost out to Cushing's chutzpah as well. The ultra-successful games sparked a worldwide interest in winter sports that continues to this day.

From the race start at the valley floor, Western States runners wind their way up to the summit of Emigrant Pass, and with Lake Tahoe at their backs, go by a rough monument of granite rock built in 1931 by Robert Montgomery Watson, the Pathfinder of the Sierra. Watson brought the Western States Trail back to life by painstakingly identifying and marking the old route that emigrants and miners had followed from Carson Valley to Auburn, which linked the silver lodes of Nevada to the gold mining camps of California. But the eager '49ers in their rough boots and with their heavily loaded horses and mules were often only following trails that had existed for centuries in the deep pine forests of the Sierra Nevada mountains.

Before them came the Washoe, Paiute, and Maidu Native Americans who had lived in the area for over a thousand years. These native peoples forged well-defined trails that led from the valleys and foothills where the tribes wintered to the high country where they enjoyed the cool lakes and alpine meadows during the summer. The mountains offered a bountiful existence. The Native Americans gathered acorns and pinyon nuts as a main staple and pulled trout out of the rivers and streams. Their homes were simple wickiups of willow poles thatched with grass, tulle, or slabs of cedar bark. The elegant and refined baskets they made are collected worldwide.

The Western States Trail area and the Native Americans living there remained undisturbed when outsiders first encroached on California. Spanish explorers kept mostly to the coast and considered California a jumping off place for trans-Pacific voyages to the Far East. Trade goods, especially cattle hides, were provided by the ranchos located just inland. The mountains beyond the great California valleys were of no interest to the Spanish who had no idea of the mineral wealth hidden there. When settlers began coming west by wagon, the Sierra Nevada were an obstacle they tried to avoid by going well north or south. Early attempts to cross directly over the mountains were often ill-fated as the Donner Party demonstrated. But things changed abruptly after January 24,

Western States runners traversing the high country early in the race

1848, when James W. Marshall, busy building a sawmill for John Sutter, came across some glittering metal. The great California Gold Rush was on.

From Emigrant Pass, the Western States trail passes through the Granite Chief Wilderness, named after a prominent rock formation, and mostly follows the Placer County Emigrant Road built in 1855 as far as Robinson Flat, a meeting place known to the Native Americans and now called the "Crossroads of the Sierra" due to the many trails that intersect there. The trail then works its way westward over Barney Cavanaugh Ridge, named after a miner responsible for the big Bonanza gold strike in the Klondike. From there runners enter the very heart of Gold Rush country, plunging in and out of a series of deep canyons. It is hard today to experience the majestic solitude and immense quietness of Deep Canyon,

Early Spanish traders kept to the coast and had no idea of the mineral wealth hidden in the mountains beyond the California valleys.

Deadwood Canyon, El Dorado Canyon, and Volcano Canyon, and appreciate what it must have been like when the area crawled with miners struck with gold fever. The roaring of water down wooden troughs, shanty towns being hammered together, noisy mules, and the cursing of the miners laboring in the hot sun would have echoed for miles up and down the canyon walls.

So many miners poured into the mountains after the first gold strike that San Francisco was practically emptied of its menfolk. In Monterey, Governor Walter Colton was said to be left governing only "a community of women, a gang of prisoners, and here and there a soldier." Within one year of the first strike, prospectors were arriving from Hawaii, Australia, Chile, and from the East Coast of the United States.

Gold Mining Towns

Key checkpoints along the Western States Trail include legendary gold mining towns. The ghost town of Last Chance is reputed to have earned its name when a group of prospectors running low on supplies sent one of the company out with a good rifle and their single remaining bullet. "This is our *last chance* to make a grubstake," he supposedly said. When he returned with a large buck, the prospectors were able to stay and make a go of the claim. Next along the trail is a bit of nature's handiwork, Devil's Thumb, a 50-foot high outcropping of volcanic rock, so named for the hellish conditions the miners often labored in. Beyond that is Deadwood, another town that sparked to life in the 1850s and then was quickly abandoned with only an old well and the small cemetery to mark its passage. Its name is said to have come from excited miners who upon making a strike boasted they had the "deadwood" on making a fortune, meaning it was a sure thing.

The town of Michigan Bluff has hung on, although at times precariously, up to the present. A picturesque jumble of houses with another Gold Rush-era cemetery right on Main Street, it had to be relocated to its present location when the original town began sliding down the mountain due to overzealous miners washing away the soil underneath it. Leland Stanford of Stanford University fame operated the general store in town and was known to sleep on the counter at night, perhaps watching over his goods. A Scotsman named Duncan Ferguson operated the trail from Last Chance to Michigan Bluff as one of America's rare toll trails. The money was used to keep the trail passable, though an occasional accident sent man or beast tumbling to an almost certain death in one of the steep canyons.

And the Last Chance Mine is still active today.

After Michigan Bluff, the trail dips through Volcano Canyon and emerges at another Gold Rush-era town, Foresthill, where the overly optimistic miners laid out a main street the width of Market Street in San Francisco in anticipation of a gold-driven metropolis. Ten million dollars' worth of gold was eventually taken out of the area "within rifle shot of the express office," but the skyscrapers never materialized. A local promontory named "Robber's Roost," where lookouts could signal how well the gold shipments were guarded, suggests that some of the gold may have been sidetracked on its way to Auburn.

No Hands Bridge

From Foresthill, the trail deviates from its traditional route through the now heavily developed Todds Valley and plunges into a canyon formed by the Middle Fork of the American River. Passing by several abandoned mine sites, the trail follows a ditch at one point that is evidence of a 1920s scheme for diverting water down to a turbine that supplied electricity to the area. The trail crosses the river at Rucky Chucky, just down river from spectacular rapids, and then before reaching Auburn, it recrosses the river at the Mountain Quarry Cement Bridge, better known to runners as "No Hands Bridge" because it once lacked a handrail. The bridge caters mostly to hikers, bikers, and Western States hundred milers today, but when it was completed in 1912, it was the longest concrete arch railroad bridge in the world and considered quite a marvel.

After crossing No Hands, the trail quickly ascends out of the river canyon to Robie Point, named after Wendell T. Robie, a member of the group that helped Watson rescue the trail from obscurity. Robie founded the Tevis Cup or Western States Trail Ride in 1955, which covers essentially the same course as the 100-mile endurance run. In fact, the run was born when Gordon Ainsleigh, a regular Tevis Cup rider, made good on his plans to forego his horse and complete the race on foot, which he did in 1974.

After Robie Point, the race course follows the streets of Auburn to its end in the stadium at Placer High School. Auburn, originally called Woods Dry Diggings and North Fork Dry Diggings, is the largest and most successful of the Gold Rush-era towns in Placer County. A huge statue commemorating French immigrant Claude Chana, who first discovered gold there in Auburn Ravine in 1848, adorns the old part of town. The ubiquitous name "Placer" comes from an American Spanish word for the deposits of sand or gravel where precious metals accumulated. Fittingly, the school, the old immigrant road, the county, various businesses, and nearby towns

Wouldn't you be dying to know the origins of the name "Scuppernong" if you passed this sign on the Ice Age Trail?

all use the name Placer and thus memorialize the miners sifting through a slurry of sand in search of those bright flakes of gold that had the power to transform a nation.

Runners in the Western States Endurance Run have a choice. They can plod along oblivious to all the landmarks, the legends, and the ghosts of those who have trod the trail before them. Or they can marvel at their remarkable visit to the storied past and perhaps catch the spirit of the Washoe Native Americans, the rugged prospectors, or the modern pioneers like Cushing, Watson, and Robie who appreciated the special value of the area and worked to preserve and share it.

But don't think that the Western States course is unique in its ability to tell a story. Any location will unfold like a storybook if you spend enough time delving into its past and learning about the people who lived there. Do a little research on the area where you normally run and train. You might be very surprised at what you discover. You might even end up imbuing your usual running routes with a little magic.

Chapter 16

Twenty-Four Hours of Attitude Adjustment

Several years ago I pulled a groin muscle badly enough that it took me completely out of running for a while. Like most runners who are forced to forego running, I saw it as the end of the world. I proceeded to rush my comeback, only to reinjure myself over and over. Eventually I wised up and realized that I had to slow down. I also needed to substitute in some other form of exercise activity or go crazy.

We had a little swimming pool in my backyard, so I splashed around in that. Meanwhile, a friend of mine talked me into buying a mountain bike and I worked on learning to ride that on the trails in a nearby park. By then, I could handle running the 5K distance as long as I didn't go too fast and kept my stride length chopped down. You see where this is going.

The glittering challenge of the triathlon lured me in. It seemed like a good fit. With the daunting task of training for three sports at once, my mind and body would be fully occupied. There would be no time to ruminate about my stalled running career. I'd be getting plenty of exercise and staying in shape. Plus the exercise would be a more comprehensive, whole-body exercise than I was getting from just running. There was even a little mini-triathlon held in San Jose about an hour from where I lived that offered me a chance to try out my new skills. The run portion was just right, a 5K, and the bike portion was staged on a ten-mile mountain bike trail. It was perfect.

The first year I competed, I couldn't swim worth a damn and came out of the water almost dead last. I was still just learning to ride the mountain bike, so I sucked at that as well. I made a little progress against the field, but I also almost wiped out a race official when I skidded through a sandy curve and almost went down. I finally got beyond the bike leg of the race and charged out of the transition area relieved to be running even though it was on my gimpy groin.

The 5K course followed the edge of a round lake so you could basically look out over the water and see all the runners ahead of you for most of the course. I caught the first runner ahead of me in no time and then the next and the next. Much to my surprise and amazement and even with the groin tugging at me, I found I was killing it. I was flying by other runners right and left. I felt like Superman.

As I sped along, dispatching this runner and then that, an explanation for my surprisingly good performance dawned on me. I was a runner first and foremost. It was my specialty. In comparison, triathletes were lousy runners. I burst across the finish line having passed something like half the competitors in

Mountain biking helped me stay in shape while recovering from the run injury.

my flight during the run. I went to check the results after cooling down and of course I was way back in the overall competition but I hadn't done too badly in my age group. It made me think that given my superior running skills, if I could just get my swim and bike legs up to moderate standards, I could place in my age group and maybe even win.

A year later I was back. The swim training had gone so-so over the course of the last year. I was a better swimmer, but I didn't care for swimming so I really hadn't done much of it. The mountain bike was a different story. I was a lot better at riding and felt like I could mix it up with anybody out there doing a triathlon. And of course I was extremely confident about my running. I wasn't back to one hundred percent, but I didn't have to run as defensively because of the groin as I had the year before.

The race began and I struggled out of the water maybe two-thirds back in the field, a lot better than the year before. I aced the transition and sped out of there on my mountain bike comfortably whipping down through the first curves of the trail. I jockeyed back and forth for position with the riders next to me and little by little moved up in the field.

Safely back at the transition area and having taken no spills off the bike, I discarded the bike shoes and slipped quickly into my running shoes. I took a long pull from a water bottle and then I was off running. Again there was a long line of runners ahead of me strung out around the lake. *Here I go*, I said to myself and put my head down and charged.

And…nothing fucking happened. I edged up on the first runner that was ahead of me, but when I drew closer, he started matching my pace. Meanwhile, we weren't making any progress at all on catching the next couple of runners farther up ahead. They were going the same speed I was going. Ditto everyone else in the race ahead of them. By halfway through the run, I'd managed to pass one or two runners but one of them passed me back.

Before reaching the finish line, I had a new revelation about my "superior" running skills. Triathletes weren't lousy runners at all as I had thought. What had happened the year before was that by doing so poorly in the swim and bike segments of the race, I had started the run segment among the least competitive triathletes in the race. They were simply as comparatively weak in the run as they had been in the swim and bike segments. Once I was up with the more accomplished triathletes during the second year, I found that their running skills were equal to or better than mine. I ended up improving my place in the overall race and within my age group but not dramatically. There was never any danger that I was going to win. My dreams of becoming a nationally prominent age group triathlon champion were dashed.

Pursuing the triathlons did, however, successfully divert a lot of my attention away from my running woes. It also gave me a break from the pressure that I was putting on myself to always run as hard as I could and go for PRs in all my races, which I was still doing back then. I was curious about how well I could do in a triathlon but I didn't really have a dog in that fight.

After my comeuppance in the triathlon world, I shifted my focus to mountain biking and that is where I really gained some perspective on how being immersed in another sport and having a whole different mindset about it can be a useful thing. I was led in that direction because of my injury, but you might consider choosing to opt out of running and spend more time in a cross-training activity if you feel burned out in your running or if the running routine has just gotten stale. Taking a break from running can give you a whole new perspective on what running means to you. You may even return to running with a renewed passion for it.

As the following account illustrates, I got into mountain biking whole hog, eventually riding with a team of guys who were strictly mountain bikers. The event we keyed on each year was called the Twenty-Four Hours of Adrenaline held at the Laguna Seca Raceway in Monterey. The story here is very true to the facts of our team's participation in the race one year, although I've assigned the team members some phony nicknames—not so much to protect the innocent as to avoid condemning the guilty.

The people, the atmosphere, the relationships, and the concerns I felt in the mountain biking world were all very different from what I had experienced as a runner. It constituted a thorough break for me from running, but at the same time kept me well trained and physically very fit. I loved the fun of it, but at the same time, as soon as my injury allowed, I transitioned back into running and perhaps took with me some attitude adjustment that I learned from being on Team Mudmen.

24 Hours of Attitude Adjustment

It's our team's third year riding together in a twenty-four hour mountain bike race and trouble is brewing. Team Mudmen has always cultivated a studied indifference to the results of the race. We're there for the fun, the camping, and the staying up all night. Oh, sure, there's the riding around on mountain bikes, but we consider that something of a necessary evil. But now we have an issue. Snake, one of our very own, actually cares how we're doing in the race.

All the signs are there. Checking his lap times. Warming up. Coming back from his loops all spent. Adjusting the air in his tires. It's sickeningly obvious. Then comes the straw that breaks the camel's back. We catch him in the results tent checking what place we're in. I start to say something to him, but I'm shouted down by the others. "We're Mudmen, damn it," they tell me. "We don't say things!" So I suck it up and keep quiet.

All I can do to deal with the problem is ride. I put in my ten-mile loops and stew. Between rides, I sit around camp focusing glumly on having fun while I graze from the mound of junk food on the picnic table.

A segment of the mountain bike course near Laguna Seca

But then Snake comes back from his loop all, "A guy got in my face! A guy wouldn't give me the trail. Some guy threw an elbow." *Who are these "guys"?* I wonder. Most riders are on teams like ours, enjoying the event and riding for the fun of it. The poor solo riders are mostly quiet, too intent on their own suffering to bother with us. Sure there's some serious competition going on, but out on the trail people are amazingly polite, especially the pros that are here, and they have the most at stake.

I get into my sleeping bag that night all bent out of shape. I really want to tell Snake off. I can imagine myself railing at him, "We've built this team up from nothing! We've done as badly as anybody out here! And now you want to compete! Compete?! The word doesn't exist in our vocabulary!"

When my turn to ride comes up, I'm fast asleep, snuggled so deep in my sleeping bag a spelunker couldn't find me.

"Your loop, Hammer King," a voice somewhere out there in the cold world says.

"Someone else go," I say through my sleeping bag material.

"It's your loop, Hammer King. Get up."

"I'm too old."

"We're all too old."

"I have nothing to wear."

"That's a laugh."

Okay, that is a laugh. Since I lack all bike-handling skills and since I also lack training, speed, and courage, I have to pretty much rely on my wardrobe to make my mark. I get up and pull out a couple of bundles of carefully packed outfits. *Hmm*...should I go with the jersey with the big pharaoh head on it or the one with the big hairy tarantula? Tough call, but I go with the spider.

My tentmate Blade is on his back snoring loudly. Blade is our ex-spook. At least we thought he was our ex-spook until he became very hard to find during the Iraq war. Now we think maybe he's our active-duty spook. Blade is all very cool about the race. He just rides and chills, which is funny because he's always the most impatient one to get going when we get together for training rides in front of my house. He pops wheelies up and down the street. He bounces off my brick wall. I'll be sitting on my bike trying to adjust my helmet straps, or I'll be stopped cold because one of my gloves has a finger inside out, and he'll have a conniption fit.

"Hold your horses," I tell him.

"Get your shit together," he'll suggest helpfully.

I pull on my spider jersey and emerge from the tent all resplendent in my get up. Out by the campfire, Slug is holding a charcoalized hotdog over the flame.

"It's two o'clock in the morning," I point out.

Slug looks up at me. "I got hungry."

Slug is our clean-up hitter. That is, he rides last because he's not too extremely fast. His training has consisted mostly of sitting on his couch and eating potato chips. We think he keeps his excuses for not riding on a Rolodex so he can just flip to the next one when we call.

Swede, the heart and soul of our team, volunteers to take me down to the transition area. He's been up all night fiddling with our bikes (a good thing in my case since I can barely change a flat). Swede, who coincidentally is from Sweden, can outride all of us, but you never hear him say a thing about it. He's not looking at lap times or making a fuss about how fast or slow anybody goes. He could fit into a much better team but he seems happy with us. "We have just fun, right?" he always says. I've been telling him about what is happening with Snake but he just puts me off. "It's cold," he says.

"You mean, 'It's cool,' right?"

"Yes, it's cool."

I put on my helmet and gloves. The gloves are still damp from my last ride. We swing over to the table where my lights are charging up. To get there, we have to cross a section of the course that cuts directly through the camping area. Riders flash by periodically, lights glaring, their knobby tires ripping at the asphalt. They sound like spaceships re-entering the atmosphere.

Swede connects up my lights for me. I walk the bike over to the transition area. *Star Wars* is playing on an enormous screen, blips and zings blaring out of a bank of speakers. A few people are sprawled on the grass watching, but mostly people are focused on the mad crush in the transition tent. Timekeepers are marking down splits on huge sheets of paper as riders leap off their bikes and run into the tent like they were announcing Armageddon, "TWENTY-EIGHT IN! TWENTY-EIGHT IN!" One of the timekeepers nods nonchalantly.

I try to stay calm by busying myself with a cup of sports drink, but all the jumpy riders waiting to go out are hyping me up. I decide it is time to recite the Mudmen creed, which I wrote myself:

We're the Mudmen, the mighty Mudmen,

Suckin' down energy gel.

We ride the night on our pricey bikes.

We're all heart and we never fail.

Bound by mud and bound by blood,

We, uh, shred the gnarly trail.

Beneath the duds and the built-up crud,

We're all heart and we never fail.

"Better you not say this thing," Swede says to me, looking around to see if anybody is listening.

Suddenly, here comes Snake tearing around the last corner of the course. He's out of his saddle, jerking his bike back and forth, and pumping furiously trying to beat the rider in front of him to the tent. A volunteer has to practically throw herself across Snake's path to get him to dismount before he takes out half the timekeepers. Even Swede looks rattled by this blatant display of machismo.

Snake extracts our baton from underneath the leg of his bike shorts and flips it to me with a sneer. "I could have beat that guy," he snarls.

I trot out to the bike racks. I momentarily dance around in circles when I can't pick my bike out of the jumble of identical bikes. I feel Snake's eyes bore into my back as I lose time. I find the bike, stow the baton in my seatpack, switch on all my lights, and hustle out of the transition area.

At this race site, just fifty yards from where the loop starts, it's necessary to get off the bike and run it over a footbridge. Riding down the steps of this bridge on the return is something of a gut check. On my first try, I bounced the handlebars of my bike up on the handrail and rode that to a momentous crash at the bottom of the steps. This was quite discouraging. Then some saint told me that riding the hard-edged steps could bend a rim. Now I run my

The dogs eagerly awaiting news on how the Mudmen performed

Our cat Bonkers seems less concerned about the performance of the Mudmen.

bike down the steps and coolly tell people, "Oh, yeah, man. You know you can bend a rim riding those steps."

The start/finish area sits down in a bowl so after the bridge it's necessary to climb out to the rest of the course. I get out of my saddle and labor up the bumpy trail. Soon I'm riding free through grassy fields studded with oak trees under a blanket of stars. I quit thinking about Snake and just cruise along, enjoying the cool night air and watching the trail rush by under my lights. I marvel in the weird sensation of being up in the middle of the night riding full tilt on a mountain bike.

My loop does not go by without mishap. I work my way down one series of tight switchbacks toward a table where volunteers are checking numbers and directing riders down the next trail. "Number 313," I yell just as I lose traction trying to make the turn. I slide directly under the table, bike and all. The volunteers scatter to save themselves.

On my way back, going up an infamous two-mile stretch of the course called "The Grind," I find I'm catching the rider in front of me. The number on the back of his seat identifies him as a solo rider. His body language as he slumps over his bike just screams pain and exhaustion. Before I reach him, though, another rider breezes by me and pulls up next to the solo guy. They talk for a minute and then I see the faster rider's hand extend out and come to rest on the small of the solo rider's back. He's helping the guy out, giving him a push up the hill.

Eventually, I make it back to the transition tent, minus a little blood. For me, any lap without a mechanical hiccough is a good lap. It takes me awhile to find the baton in my seatpack. It's lost among old energy bar wrappers and disintegrated tire tube boxes. Slug is waiting, ready to go. He's already beet red from the effort of…what...walking his bike over here? I give him the baton and he lumbers off toward the bike racks.

The moments after a night loop are magical. I float along in an easy gear through a quiet camp. Muffled voices issue from a few tents. A fire crackles here and there. On the hillside above me, lights appear from time to time and zigzag down the hill.

I roll into camp. My brakes emit a high-pitched squeal as I stop. I duck into the tent. "We own the night, man!" I yell.

"Get the hell out of here, you idiot. This isn't your tent."

I go find the correct tent. "We own the night, man!" I yell.

"It's not my turn, you idiot. Go find Swede."

Swede is huddled with Snake next to the dying embers of the fire. It looks like they're having a heart to heart. "How did lap go?" Swede asks.

"Cleaned it," I say in my best shorthand mountain bike lingo.

"I am telling to Snake," Swede looks up at me and telecasts the biggest secret wink I have ever seen in my life, "how I am thinking. He might like solo riding next year instead of bad team."

"Oh, yeah," I say, catching on immediately. "Those solo guys look like they're having all the fun."

“What about the team?” Snake asks.

“Don’t worry. Mudmen okay. It’s cold,” Swede says. “We can find submarine for you.”

“Substitute,” I suggest.

Snake kicks at the edge of the fire. “Yeah, maybe I’ll ride solo next year,” he says finally.

Soon I’m burrowing back into my sleeping bag with a lightened heart. It appears that the Mudmen will be restored to their rightful position in the pantheon of totally indifferent mountain bike teams. We will ride, oblivious to the tyranny of lap times and the overlordship of the results tent. We may never place in the top half of the field but we will enjoy ourselves and eat heartily.

Oh, yes, and ride our expensive bikes around in the moonlight.

Epilogue

The Cool-Down

Let's recap. Running is a completely awesome and cool activity. It's wonderfully rewarding, builds your self-esteem, keeps you healthy, and helps you understand just who you are and where you're going in life. These rewards, though, don't just fall in your lap. Running can be difficult especially if you're pushing yourself and reaching for challenging goals.

When the going gets tough, you quickly realize that your mental attitude and your mental resources are going to be the keys to your success as a runner, and that the personal growth you experience through running happens within your mind. In fact, the mental side of running is fascinating in and of itself and leads you to know thyself and know what you're capable of. Two critical mental resources that you will need to cultivate are patience and determination. These two qualities allow you to keep your thinking positive and to push through challenges that seem insurmountable.

It is the overcoming of hard challenges and the reaching of lofty goals that lead to much of the self-satisfaction that you derive from running. Falling short of a goal can lead to even greater rewards when you pick yourself up, come back, and achieve the goal that frustrated you before.

Practicing mindfulness as you run helps you better sink down into your running experience and appreciate it more. It will also provide you with some very effective techniques for pain management. In addition to practicing mindfulness, mindful running includes being aware of different mental frameworks or states of mind that can structure or affect your thinking as you run. You can cycle through the techniques of the four horsemen of the apocalypse: mindfulness, mantras, music, and moxie. You can laugh and joke your way to the finish. You can experience your route as an unfolding storybook. You can be your dog. Exhaustion can visit upon you visions and bizarre fantasies. You can stay positive, elude the negative, and remain strictly in the moment.

I hope after reading this book that you think of running as a huge mind game, fascinating and very rewarding to explore, and that you see your whole experience of running as a journey both in the world and through your own mental landscape.

So be a mindful runner and find your inner focus. What will you discover within? What will you learn about yourself?

Postscript

If you found this book interesting and useful, be sure to seek out my other book on running, *The Tao of Running: Your Journey to Mindful and Passionate Running*. It will complete the picture on the possibilities of finding your inner focus. Tell your runner friends about these books and don't hesitate to go to Amazon and leave a quick review. All feedback is welcome. See you out on the roads, footpaths, and trails!

You've just got to find your inner focus...

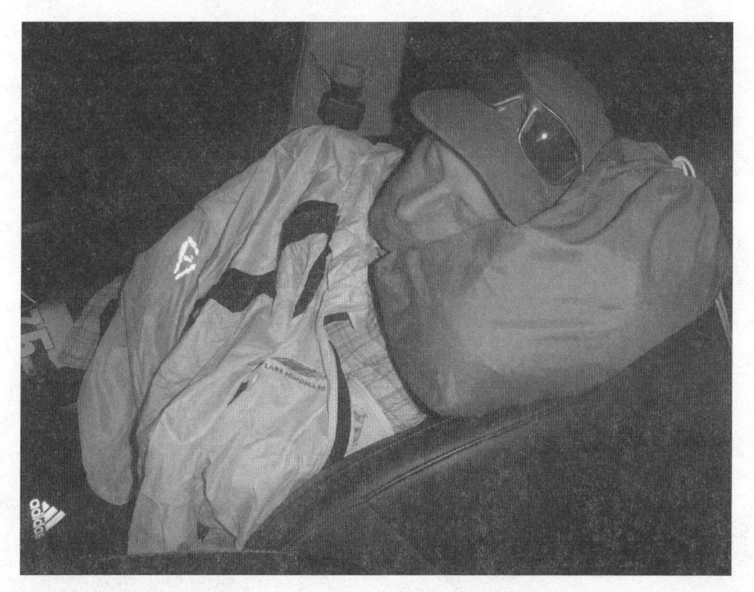

...then you can relax.

Credits

Design & Layout

Cover and Interior Design: Anja Elsen
Layout: Amnet

Photos & Illustration

Cover Illustration: © AdobeStock
Interior Photos: All photos © Gary Dudney, unless otherwise noted

Editorial

Managing Editor: Elizabeth Evans
Copyeditor: Anne Rumery

MORE GREAT RUNNING BOOKS

304 p., b/w, 45 photos,
paperback,
5.5" x 8.5"
ISBN: 9781782550754
$14.95 US

Gary Dudney

THE TAO OF RUNNING

YOUR JOURNEY TO MINDFUL
AND PASSIONATE RUNNING

The Tao of Running offers a fresh perspective on the mental side of running. It shows you how to use mindfulness to reduce tension in your life, to stay positive no matter how tough the challenge, and to run with passion. Going well beyond the standard training and racing advice found in most running books, it answers questions such as: How does running lead to stress reduction? How does it fit into your own aspirations, goals, and life philosophy?

No other book offers these multiple frameworks for understanding your running experiences along with lots of practical advice on getting the most out of running. You are guaranteed to gain a greater appreciation for the rewards and possibilities inherent in running and will significantly deepen, enlighten, and enrich your running experience.

Make an adventure out of every run and learn to use running to improve and transform your life!

FROM MEYER & MEYER SPORT